AND THEN YOU WENT MISSING

A Hope-Filled Guide for Anyone Lost in a Difficult Relationship

Sonja Meyrer

And Then You Went Missing

Printed in the United States of America

Hamburg Nord Publishing

Copyright © 2023 by Sonja Meyrer

Feelings Wheel printed with permission from leadskill.com.

Scripture quotes marked ESV are from the ESV Bible (The Holy Bible, English Standard Version), copyright @ 2001 by Crossway, a publishing ministry of Good New Publishers.

ISBN: 9798367280906

First Edition 2023

Cover Design: @nskvsky

Author Image: Shannon Worley

Illustrations: Grace Radke

Book Coaching: Michelle M. Cox

Marketing: Deanna McClintock

For Lucas, Devin and Siena

4 Forever

contents

Foreward

As a professional therapist, I often work with clients who appear to have gotten lost in relationships that overwhelm them with fear or frustration. Helping people forge a path forward out of unhealthy dependency takes time and patience but it is well worth the effort. I have seen people turn their lives around and find the healing and health they long for. Sometimes, a client will ask for a practical book or resource to accelerate their growth and help them take concrete steps forward. But one of my frustrations with "self-help" books is that many authors fill most of the pages by defining the problem and they spend little time on solutions.

This is NOT that kind of book.

From the beginning the author walks you through steps that quickly become building blocks that will truly create healthy relational movement in your life. This is a book rich with practical insight that you will be able to apply in your life **today**.

I'm excited for you, the reader, that you are about to embrace this book. You will not just read it and set it aside, you will linger over certain parts, because they apply so directly to something you are currently experiencing. You will want to share it with friends because it will touch on an area that you know will help them. I encourage you to save it in your device or find a place on your bookshelf because you will be looking for it in the future to re-read a chapter or reflect on a question that is asked.

Why? Wisdom.

The deepest part of wisdom comes from the decisions we make in response to the pain we have in life. I have walked with the author through some of the most painful days of her life. What I observed, and continue to observe, is someone who took those moments of agony, that we all have, and turned them into compassion and practical care for others. I have seen the author over and over ask two questions, many times without even realizing it:

What can I learn from this?

How can I give to others using this?

That passion is reflected on each page. It creates a depth and a richness that does not just parrot something she learned from her education; it showcases a true desire to help others.

So, you're welcome.

Why do I say that? Because when you get to the end of this book you will come back to this introduction to remember my name and say, "That guy was right! This one is a keeper."

And you will be right!

Jeff L. Taylor LPC, Co-owner, Chesterfield Counseling Associates

Preface

The idea for writing this book came on the heels of a workshop I offer called Boundaries in Relationships. A participant thought that her friend "really needed to hear about boundaries too" and she wanted to know if I had I ever considered writing a book. Surely, other people who were lost in unhealthy relationships could benefit from the things we had discussed. Maybe I could expand on the class workbook and publish something for a broader audience?

Her request intrigued me. I had published several blogs for our counseling center and created content and curriculum for many years. (And my sister-in-law always praised my Christmas letters!) But writing a book would be a much bigger and more terrifying commitment. Plenty of experts had produced material on codependency, emotional health, and boundaries, so pulling together relevant information would not be a problem. But I would need to infuse the chapters with real-life stories in order for the content to come alive; stories from clients, friends, family and, of course, from my own journey. Would my family be in favor of such a project? Could I protect the identities of my clients? Was I willing to open up about the years *I went missing* and the painstaking journey to reclaim my identity and my life? For this book to be credible, I knew I really did not have a choice.

A few months after the seed was planted, I quit my full-time job and amended my LinkedIn profile to read, "Sonja Meyrer, author." My amazing book coach walked me through the writing process, forcing me to think hard about what I knew, believed, and wanted to communicate. Looking back over my own inventory of dysfunctional relationships and codependent behaviors was quite humbling, to be sure. I laughed aloud, cringed, rolled my eyes and asked myself a dozen times, "What were you thinking?" Some people in these stories still push my buttons, while some are no longer a part of my journey at all. Others came into my life during a specific "season" and then exited, leaving their rich contribution impressed upon my soul.

In the chapters of this book, you will bear witness to the stories of struggle and healing taken from the lives of ordinary people. The names and details have often been changed, but the integrity of the events remains the same. My family has kindly allowed me to share a few very personal experiences as well. Thank you in advance for approaching their stories with grace and respect.

In these chapters you will, from time to time, hear me share about my faith. I have chosen to do so because God is woven into the fabric of my life and to remove him from these pages would be inauthentic. But I wrote this book for anyone of any faith, including those who profess no religion at all. While we all have unique experiences and perspectives, what we have in common is the pursuit of healthy relationships in a flourishing life.

IntroDuction

"Her eyes gave her away. There was a drowning girl behind that smile." - *Atticus.*

Growing up in the 70s, when gluten and lactose were still regarded with affection, a bowl of sugary cereal swimming in homogenized milk was a breakfast staple for many families, including my own. On weekends, my brothers and I would bounce into the kitchen, pour ourselves a generous heap of charms, flakes or pops and then line up the boxes on the kitchen counter. The five of us took turns reading the jokes and solving the puzzles on the back. Each one of us had our own unique ritual for consumption; the younger boys, whose lives seemed to be centered on perpetual competition, would devour as much of every type of cereal as quickly as they could. With a slight air of sisterly superiority, I showed more restraint by first nibbling away at the sensible brown and gold pieces, leaving the colorful marshmallows and berries until the end. Our older brother did not commit to any of these practices, choosing instead to experiment from week to week with different combinations of cereal and quantities of milk. Save for the occasional dispute over extracting and allocating the prizes inside the boxes, these mornings were sacred to our little posse. I suspect that many other children growing up in that era were enjoying a similar experience.

But a decade later, something frightening and slightly sinister infiltrated these breakfast routines all over the country. Juxtaposed with the cheery pictures of leprechauns and tigers on the cereal boxes, kids in the 80s were often confronted with a black-and-white image of a missing child on the side of their milk carton. For those of you who were born into the digital age, these somewhat shocking advertisements served as a primitive version of an Amber Alert. They featured a head shot of the missing child, their physical description, and the name of the person they were last seen with.

While the campaign did reunite some children with their families, it was discontinued a decade later. Researchers and pediatricians spoke out about its effect on other children who were becoming terrified at the prospect of going missing themselves. I can only imagine what young children must have been thinking as they stared at the images of boys and girls who were now "nowhere to be found." *Did they wander off at a department store and have to spend the night under a rack of dresses? Did someone take them by accident and will they give them back? What if they are cold or dirty, sad or scared, thirsty or hungry? Will somebody take me?*

As an adult thinking back on those missing faces, I sense the weight of the tremendous loss that would accompany such an incident; loss of control, loss of connection, loss of physical touch. I cannot imagine how I would function if someone I loved would disappear. But it also occurred to me that people can go missing in other ways; even when they are still physically present. When we are burdened by circumstances, unwanted changes, or pressures, we might be prone to emotionally and mentally "check out." When we engage in risky or addictive behaviors, we might say or do things that leave our baffled friends wondering, "Who are you?" Or, when we are stuck in an unhealthy relationship, consumed with worry, anger or fear, we might lose our joy, our passions and our self-esteem. We might become a shadow of the person we used to be.

An Exasperated Mother

Cathy walked into our first coaching session with a pained look on her face: her eyes were glassy, her brows furrowed, and her lips pressed tightly against each other. Tall and sinewy - her hair pulled back into a no-nonsense ponytail - she looked surprisingly frail. It was easy to see that she had a lot on her mind. She had never been to see a mental health professional before, and she was uncomfortable with letting someone have a peek into her personal life. However, her sister persuaded her to "talk to someone" about her relationship with her drug-addicted son. At the end of her rope (and tired of her sibling's nagging), she obliged.

According to her family, Cathy was a hard-working, competent and loving single mother of four who had overcome many difficulties in her life with great strength and determination. A talented musician and vocalist, she taught piano and voice lessons during the day and played in various bands on weekends to support herself. Fourteen months prior to our meeting, her adult son had moved back home after several failed attempts at addiction treatment. Recently, he had been resuscitated in the emergency room after a near-fatal drug overdose. Jobless and penniless, Cathy's son spent most of his time sleeping, playing video games, and partying with friends. Despite his mother's desperate pleas to "clean up his act," he seemed unmotivated to look for work, get sober, or take ownership of his life.

Cathy knew she was enabling her son by allowing him to stay in her home, but she was also terrified that his next overdose might kill him. By having him live with her, she could at least make sure he was breathing, eating, and somewhat safe. But as she became more and more consumed with trying to manage her son's life, Cathy became less and less interested in investing in her own. She often canceled her lessons and weekend gigs and began dipping into her retirement funds to make up for lost income. Consumed with constant anxiety and worry, Cathy rarely slept more than a few hours at a time and she frequently forgot to eat. Many of her friends had stopped reaching out to invite her places, and she avoided most family gatherings altogether. Her brain seemed perpetually foggy and she sometimes struggled to string a coherent sentence together. In her own words, Cathy felt lost and unsure of how to find her way back.

Could You Be Missing, Too?

Have you ever been lost in a difficult relationship? In your attempts to manage or control the life of someone else, have you ever forgotten to care about your own? Have you become so habitually focused on understanding the feelings and behaviors of other people that you no longer trust your own thoughts and opinions? Then take note, my dear reader: You may not find your face on a milk carton but it is still possible that you have "gone missing."

You may not have a family member struggling with the disease of addiction, but you might still recognize yourself somewhere in Cathy's story. Is there someone you desperately want to change, control, or fix? Do you ever modify your behavior or compromise your values to accommodate the issues or difficult personality of someone else? If you picked up this book, chances are that there might be a family member, friend or colleague who "pushes your buttons" or consumes an inordinate amount of your thoughts or time. Sometimes we can brush off the issues and personality quirks of others, but other times it's not so easy. Consider these relational conundrums:

- Perhaps you have a hot-tempered spouse who reacts to stress with angry outbursts. She has many redeeming and wonderful qualities, but to manage her volatility you say (or don't say) things to preempt a "flare up." Often you tolerate tone and language that you would otherwise find unacceptable.

- Or you may have a daughter who is making poor choices, getting into trouble, or hanging out with an unsavory crowd. In your embarrassment or shame over her behavior, you make excuses for her, let her get away with things and underplay the gravity of her issues.

- Possibly you have a friend or family member who leans on you a lot and seems to need you at all hours of the day without reciprocation or even thanks. You inwardly frown when you see a text from her, but you feel guilty about letting her down. So, you often spend your free time "talking her off the ledge" and ignoring the things you wanted to get done.

How to Boil a Frog

Difficult people, like the ones in the examples above, are not always acting out of malicious intent. Life is hard, people struggle and sometimes when they are under too much stress, they "leak" and allow their emotions to spill over onto others (hence the saying, "hurt people hurt people"). An angry spouse may be letting off steam created in her toxic work environment. Poor self-esteem may be at the root of a teenager's run-in with the law. A depressed friend may be so emotionally overwhelmed that he seems not to care about your life at all.

Our response to people in these situations will vary depending on the depth and nature of the relationship. A spouse's frustration over losing a job can evoke a stronger sense of compassion or urgency than a neighbor's missing cat. Most of us instinctively want to listen, help and problem-solve wherever possible. At times, we might temporarily put our own needs aside or forge the path of least resistance to move a relationship into a more peaceful and productive space. Even if it may cost us something (monetarily or otherwise) or cause us temporary discomfort, caring for others is essential for the wellbeing of our families, our communities and for the whole of humanity.

Yet, as the above examples attest, sometimes we cross over into an uncomfortable place where we *habitually:*

- Say "yes" to things when we want to say "no"

- Take responsibility for other people's struggles because we blame ourselves

- Tolerate unkind or unacceptable behaviors

- Become increasingly resentful about picking up the pieces for someone else *over and over again*

At times, we might find that our participation in unhealthy or damaging patterns has left us demoralized, speechless, or defenseless.

Maybe you have heard the fable about the frog that jumps into a pot of water. If the water is hot, the frog will jump out instinctively, knowing it is in danger. But, if the water is comfortable, the frog may choose to stay in. If someone turns up the flame just a little, the frog will not notice the change or know that it is in danger. Unfortunately, by the time the water gets hot, the poor amphibian will be too "cooked" to jump out.

Like the frog, we might automatically push back on a hostile person or quickly remove ourselves from an abusive situation. But repeatedly tolerating or giving in to smaller transgressions (like swearing, criticizing, blaming) can still be damaging. At some point, we may not even notice how calloused or oblivious we have become to our own needs. We might find ourselves in "boiling water" without even knowing it.

(In Chapter Two, we will talk more about how to recognize these kinds of harmful behaviors.)

The Myth of Control

Outside of severing our ties to humanity (or opting for a solitary life on a ranch in Montana) what can we do to get people to stop hurting us or making us angry? How can we get them to change?

In a nutshell, we can't.

We have no control over other people, their behaviors or their decisions. Unless we restrain, manipulate or trick them, other people are free to do as they please.

Yet the beautiful flip side to that harsh reality is this: **We can change**. *We* can learn to adapt and then control our own reactions and responses. *We* can challenge our old beliefs and forge new pathways. In fact, (borrowing this from a counselor friend) we are ridiculously in charge of ourselves.

Early on, Cathy had convinced herself that she could not leave her son to his own devices. She was terrified that she might come downstairs and find him unresponsive, or that an officer might knock on her door in the middle of the night to report that her boy had died of an overdose. So, she did what she thought any caring mother should do and tried to manage his life. She waited until he was asleep and then disposed of his drug paraphernalia. She tried to find him a job. She lectured, begged and pleaded with him to get help. And time and time again, she would fall into the trap of believing him when he said he would change. In reality, he had no intention of ever doing so.

During one of our early meetings, Cathy acknowledged her powerlessness over her son and her inability to get him to do anything different. She knew she needed to stop obsessing over him in order to find some peace in her own life, but several questions still loomed: How could she find peace in a situation that was unbearable for her to watch? How could she just ignore his behavior and pretend that it didn't bother her? If she chose "tough love" and kicked him out, would she be able to live with herself? In the sessions that followed we addressed each of these questions and slowly, she saw how her obsession with solving her son's problems was hurting both of them.

She learned to practice acceptance, detachment and setting boundaries. (We will talk about these in the chapters to come.) She made a conscious choice to turn her thoughts to other things and matters at hand. As her obsession and confusion dissipated, something miraculous happened: Cathy found a bit of joy again. It started with the color returning to her face, which was followed by the steady emergence of her wonderful smile. The anxious, defeated woman who sat on the sofa wringing her hands was now talking animatedly about her love of teaching and the funny antics of her students.

Cathy made a choice. While she loved her son very much, she no longer would allow his problems to hijack her life. She took a leap of faith and decided that she mattered too. Can you identify with Cathy? Have you put your life on hold while trying to fix, control, or manage someone else's life for them?

Are you ready for something new?

Ready or Not

When Cathy first asked, "What can I do?" I countered with, "Are you ready for change?" The tools for reclaiming our lives and setting boundaries within our relationships are available to us, and we can learn and practice them. *But* the process will cost us something as we surrender old habits and risk doing something new. Often, we delay pursuing change until we are out of other options. Only when the status quo becomes intolerable are we ready to do something new.

As you read this book, you will want to ask yourself how tolerable your status quo is and how willing you are to embrace change.

Even when we are unhappy with a current situation, we may not always be ready to "do" something about it right away. Like the frog in the warm water, we may be so accustomed to the temperature that we don't feel any urgency to "hop out of the pot."

In coaching, we use the **Behavioral Change Model** to assess someone's willingness or readiness to change or take action. There are six steps in the full model, but the first four (as illustrated) are most useful in discussing personal or relational change.

PRE-CONTEMPLATION   CONTEMPLATION   DETERMINATION   ACTION

Here are the phases that typically come before the Action stage:

1. Pre-Contemplation In this stage, we might be uncomfortable with a particular issue or frustrated by someone's behavior but not yet ready to address any problems or do anything different. We might be confused, in denial or just not motivated.

2. Contemplation Here we might feel convicted to change but not yet ready to do so. We might be exploring our options or seeking advice, but only in theory. No concrete plans have been laid out yet.

3. Determination A precursor to taking action, in this stage, we find ourselves unhappy with the status quo and make a decision to do something different.

When the stakes are high and there is the potential for loss of relationship involved, we might spend years contemplating and considering change before we are ready to take action. But when the motivation hits us, or we cannot tolerate the way a relationship is making us feel any longer, we can move through these three stages rather quickly. Or we might skip them altogether.

Making it Personal

You may have heard the term "hitting rock bottom" used to describe this place of intolerance. In the rooms of recovery (like Alcoholics Anonymous or Al-Anon) we often refer it to as a point of "incomprehensible demoralization"–a time when our life has become so unmanageable that we have to do something different.

My personal rock bottom took place while looking into the actual bottom of a tall, blue recycling bin. It was a sweltering summer day, and I had been up early waiting for my husband to leave for work so I could creep into the garage and do some reconnaissance work. I flung open the sturdy receptacle and stuck my head precariously far inside, the tips of my hair soaking in the disgusting gray liquid that had accumulated at the bottom. The bin was filled with cardboard, empty cans and bottles, and it reeked of warm beer and coffee. It was repulsive and I wanted to vomit, but I was not daunted because I was on a mission. I was going to count the number of beer bottles my husband had emptied in the last twelve hours and present him with the evidence so that he would finally admit he had a problem with alcohol.

His drinking had been a sore spot in our relationship for a few years. In earlier times we had both enjoyed an occasional drink when the situation called for it: a toast to a special event, a cool refresher after a long day of work, a fashionable cocktail when out with friends. But one day that changed. In the middle of the week, after a stressful day at work, my husband walked in the door, dropped his bag on the ground, took a glass out of the liquor cabinet and poured himself a drink. A real drink. I believe it was whiskey, but I can't be sure. He didn't offer me any. He just emptied the glass and sighed. And then it happened again and again. There were more drinks on more occasions, there was more sighing, and everywhere we went alcohol was now a part of our entourage. I pointed this out to him on many occasions, but these conversations got us nowhere. He accused me of being a critical, ungrateful wife, and I let him know how selfish and thoughtless he was behaving.

But I was convinced that he would not push back when I presented him with hard evidence, in the form of empty beer bottles, of just how much he was drinking. With my bare hands, I pushed the lighter recycling items to the side and I began counting: one, two, three...... eight, nine, ten. I could sense the cortisol coursing through my body as I looked down in shock and disbelief. Who could drink ten bottles of beer in one night and not admit they had a problem? Just last week he had promised (again) to cut back! I felt mocked, defeated and disregarded. A wave of panic settled in as I considered what else he might have been hiding from me. Despite all the things I wanted to accomplish that day, I knew from experience that I would spend the greater part of my time obsessing about my findings and thinking of ways to confront him.

After taking a few pictures, I righted myself in the stiflingly humid garage and it suddenly hit me like a ton of bricks. What was I doing? Did I just search for my sanity in a recycling bin? How had my life become so out of control? Did I need photographic evidence to prove that something was wrong? I didn't know what to do next, but I was sure that another confrontation was not the answer. I knew something had to change, and I was finally ready to do something different.

About This Book

Even if you are still hesitant about your ability to set boundaries and change your relationships, I am confident this book can help you take steps toward leading a more serene life and finding a new or renewed sense of self. In Chapter One we will see what research has to say about the benefits of healthy relationships. In Chapters Two-Three, we will take an in-depth look at the factors that contribute to frustrating or difficult relationships. In Chapters Four-Nine, we will explore some important tools that will help us become more self-aware and begin implementing changes and setting boundaries to protect what we value. I share the conclusion of my personal journey in an alcoholic marriage in the Epilogue.

Each chapter will conclude with reflection questions to help you apply the material to your own life. Consider reading this book with a few friends or colleagues and working through the questions during a weekly study. Use the QR code at the end of each chapter to access additional resources related to the topic.

By the end of the book, you may well be ready to stand up, speak out, and set boundaries to protect what is most important to you. And if you sense you have gone missing, it is my deepest desire that you will take delight in your own re-discovery and then give yourself permission to live an authentic, joy-filled life.

Two Important Assumptions

One last word. In order for this book to be useful, I would like us to agree on two very basic assumptions (or at least be open to the possibility they may be true). Those are:

1. You do not need permission to take ownership of your life.

You already have it. If you are unhappy with your status quo and want to have better relationships, it is entirely up to you to initiate change. Even those of us who look to God for discernment and guidance carry the responsibility for growth squarely on our own shoulders.

2. You matter.

Not only do you matter, but your words and actions matter too. I am convinced that the God who knows and cares about you created you for a purpose. He gave you gifts and talents to be shared with the people in your orbit. When you allow yourself to be sucked up into someone else's negative "stuff" or you repeatedly sacrifice your emotional, spiritual or physical well-being while trying to regulate someone else's emotions, you cannot bring your full self to the table. Or worse, your seat may be vacant altogether.

When you go missing, the world is missing out on you!

CHAPTER 1

Wired For Relationship

"You are my greatest adventure." - *The Incredibles*

Mary is one of my besties. Though my kids would roll their eyes and beg me to never use the word "bestie," for the life of me I cannot think of a better one. Although I have only known Mary for a handful of years, it feels like we have been friends forever. What our relationship might lack in time, it makes up for in substance and quality. Through a bunch of different life seasons we have challenged each other to grow, supported each other through devastating losses, and celebrated when God orchestrated things in our favor. Most of the time, though, we just talk. On the phone, over coffee, on the lanai of her Florida condo - we chat about cooking, parenting, racism, gardening, God, sex, books and podcasts. Besides pondering major life events, we try to keep each other abreast of the everyday minutia and the very average happenings in our respective worlds.

Mary also cares for me in tangible and practical ways. The last time she showed up at my house, she lugged in a huge tote, plopped it onto the counter and ceremoniously unpacked an array of goodies. She pulled out a tall container of fresh gazpacho, a still warm pot of stew, a loaf of homemade bread, a bottle of wine, and at least a dozen chewy brownies. Next to the food she assembled a bouquet of flowers picked from her own yard. To punctuate the end of the gift giving, she handed me a jar of Masala curry paste she had used in an Indian recipe. She just "knew" how much I would love it.

Not only do I delight in the support and sustenance Mary provides, but I also relish knowing that she loves to be there for me. When I gush and thank her, she waves a hand dismissively and tells me not to be silly. "It's nothing and you would do the same for me," she always says. But those words are more charitable than true. This friend thinks ahead about how to care and show her affection for me. And in her company, I feel like the most important person in her world.

I need good people in my life; I thrive when I do. But you may not have a friend like Mary. You may prefer to keep company with folks of fewer words or ones blessed with other talents. Or you might be done with people altogether, preferring not to let anyone get too close again. I get it. I have seen my fair share of unhealthy relationships as well. If you are anything like me, the negative memories of the "not-so-good" interactions are visceral, and they can evoke powerful emotions long after they have occurred. I can still recall the betrayal I felt when a popular 5th grade girl convinced our entire class not to vote for me in our homeroom elections. That was over forty years ago! I remember the pain of breaking up with my first boyfriend, disappointing my math teacher and being criticized by the parents of an unhappy student. Even today

I get nauseated recalling the sound of my abusive step-father's car pulling into our driveway.

Relationships Basics

Despite the pain they can cause, people still matter in our lives and science would support that claim. Across a variety of disciplines, our biological and psychological need for human connection is well-researched and, in fact, quite astounding. Humans arrive on this earth hard-wired and pre-programmed for relationships and our personality and character develop over our lifetime in the context of social interactions. Some of our deepest needs include being seen, valued and loved by other people. As we age, our interactions with others help us develop our passions, form our opinions, evaluate our circumstances, and surmount various obstacles.

As a collective society, we also benefit from our social interactions as we collaborate, critique, and challenge each other. Biological anthropologist Dr. Michael Platt points out, "(our) social behavior is a critical part of our adaptive toolkit. It allows us to come together and do things we wouldn't be able to do on our own."[1]

In this chapter, we will look at four important truths about relationships:

1. They set a foundation.

2. They help us grow.

3. They support healing.

4. They provide opportunities to love.

1. Relationships set a foundation.

From a developmental standpoint, the research is conclusive. Our formative relationships with our earliest caregivers can lay a foundation for safety and security - or a lack thereof - for the rest of our lives. Infants who are loved and nurtured, who feel safe and seen and who know that their basic needs will be consistently met by a human who delights in them, will have a far greater chance of developing into healthy, productive adults. Most often, these children will develop a "secure attachment style," meaning they allow themselves to be comforted by their caregiver knowing there is someone to rely on. In turn, they feel more confident interacting with and exploring the world around them. By contrast, children who experience rejection or inconsistency may develop unhealthy attachment styles leading to anxious, avoidant and clingy behaviors.[2]

Research is also clear that these early relational experiences have long-lasting implications for our long-term mental health. The Minnesota Longitudinal Study of Risk and Adaptation (a 35-year study of human development) revealed that children with a "secure attachment history" (as described above) were more likely to develop strengths that would last through a lifetime in areas such as:

- emotional regulation,

- coping with stress,

- maintaining friendships and romantic relationships,

- higher self-esteem.[3]

Interestingly, these results were consistent across a variety of cultures and despite socio-economic differences.

In witnessing this kind of attachment behavior, I am fascinated with (and squeamish about) the 1975 "Still Face Experiment" conducted and captured on video by professor and researcher Dr. Ed Tronick.[4] In the first moments of the footage, the viewer observes what appears to be a loving interaction between a young mother and her infant, full of smiles, cooing and sweet mutual adoration. Although the child is restrained in a high chair, she appears happy and enthusiastic about spending time with her beloved mom. Within a short period, however, the mother switches gears, putting on a "still" or emotionless face and for a few minutes her child enters a state of physical and emotional distress. The baby repeatedly tries to get her mother's attention, reaches for her, cries and then thrashes about when she cannot. At the end of the experiment, the mother switches back to the role of nurturing caregiver and quickly soothes the child. (And the viewer can breathe a sigh of relief.)

Why does this matter? For some of us, secure attachment in our formative years provided by loving parents and/or other caregivers supplied the foundation and safety to explore and develop other important relationships later in life. Those of us who experienced love and acceptance as children are prone to look for (or even expect) these same values to be present in our friendships and later in our romantic relationships. For those of us who did not experience secure attachment as children, the opposite might be true. It does not take an advanced degree in developmental psychology to understand how a child who habitually experiences emotional inconsistency (like in "the Still Face" experiment) might develop serious relational issues later in life.

Repeated Patterns

My client, Paul, was the only son of an immigrant family that had moved to Brooklyn when he was six. His parents worked hard to provide for his physical needs, but they had little time or capacity for supporting him emotionally or for providing physical love. Paul was expected to do well in school, keep out of trouble and help with the family business when possible. Perpetually concerned about money, Paul's father often blamed his wife for mismanaging their finances. As a result, she struggled with bouts of severe depression, often spending hours sitting alone in the kitchen staring out at the window. Paul did his best to support his mom, often taking over household chores and getting her up in the morning and into bed at night.

As Paul matured, he vowed to do things differently with his own family. He went to college and worked hard to make sure that finances were never an issue. His steady income afforded his children opportunities that he never had, such as club soccer and private dance lessons. Wanting to be more present than his own dad, Paul faithfully attended his children's events, made sure the family got to church on Sundays and took his family on extravagant vacations.

But Paul's wife was unhappy in their marriage. She felt lonely and disconnected from her husband and wished they could spend more time talking, going for walks, or laughing together. In her experience, Paul was excelling at being a good caretaker but struggling to be intimate or vulnerable. When she shared this with him, he was taken aback. How could she ask even more of him? Did she not see how hard he was trying? To his credit, Paul agreed to see a marriage counselor with his wife and over time he came to understand what she was craving. Although their weekly sessions were sometimes painful and confusing, Paul learned he did not know how to be emotionally intimate or connect with his wife on that level because he had not experienced the unconditional love and nurture he needed as a child. He truly wanted to be more open and emotional with his wife but, he simply did not know how.

We will talk more about our family of origin in Chapter Three. Spoiler alert: we *can* learn to change and heal!

2. Relationships help us grow.

As we age, our brains continue to absorb all of our relational experiences and work to make sense of our environment, keep us safe and alive, and help us develop and manage our ever-expanding competencies and responsibilities. We owe much of our understanding of this phenomenon to the enormous contributions of neuroscience. The media outlets are awash in buzz words like "plasticity," "synapses" and "neural pathways." Celebrities like Oprah and Michael Phelps speak openly about the importance of understanding our brains in order to thrive. Images of the brain are being used to teach children and adults alike how to understand their feelings and manage ongoing struggles with issues like anxiety and depression. Advanced technologies like the EEG, MRI, CT and SPECT scans have been especially fruitful in helping us bring long-lasting healing to those who suffer from trauma, addiction and mental illness.

As you might have guessed, brain science has much to say about the significance of relationships for our continued development. Dr. Daniel Siegel, a researcher and professor of Psychiatry at UCLA, is the founder of an integrative study of the mind called Interpersonal Neurobiology (IPNB) which examines the relationship between our experiences as humans and the growth of the brain. Besides supporting the attachment theory mentioned above, Dr. Siegel concludes this about relationships:

- The relationships we have with others shape our brains. Our ability to self-examine comes AFTER we have been exposed to relationships.

- Our continued relational experiences shape our neural architecture — that is to say, our social interactions are one of the most important contributors in literally forming who we are.

- The "mirror neurons" in our brains that reflect what we are experiencing through others are always at work, providing information about the people closest to us and their feelings. (This shows the science behind the "Still Face Experiment" mentioned earlier.) If we mindfully seek supportive (healthy) relationships, our brains will respond and we will grow new (healthy) neural pathways.[5]

What does this tell us? In a nutshell, that **our brains are perpetually teachable**. They can heal, reshape, and restructure with positive, meaningful interaction. For the rest of our lives, we can learn and "unlearn." If we want to become more self-aware, understand our emotions and reactions and eventually extend that understanding to those we care about, the solitary life on the secluded ranch in Montana is not the right approach, at least not for the long haul.

3. Relationships support healing.

In my experience, one of the most important reasons for having loving people in our lives is the healing power of relationships. Of course, this is not a new concept by any means, and no one has understood it better than the artistic community. Songwriters have been crooning about the restorative benefits of friendship and romantic love for decades. As Marvel fans can attest, even the latest Spider-Man release brought the three latest versions of the human arachnid together for mutual support and healing. Alice Lesperance writes in praise of the message of healing and friendship in the Harry Potter series, "... the novels reminded me I'm not going mad, or that if I am, someone else probably is, too. The pain in those middle books is so visceral and familiar, but as I keep reading, I remember that the last moments we spend with Harry in those final books are all about fighting on and holding tightly to hope—together."[6]

In their timely and important book, *SEEN - Healing Despair and Anxiety in Kids and Teens Through the Power of Connection*, the authors recognize the powerful difference an adult can make by regularly showing up for a child.[7] While there is no simple answer for combating depression or thoughts of suicide among our youth, simple practices can make a difference:

- Show up consistently.

- Look them in the eye and see them for who they really are.

- Listen well.

- Speak life-giving words.

- Help them develop grit to get through difficult times.

I would like to propose, however, that those are not just tools for helping to heal our kids. Think about how it feels when someone keeps in touch with you through a tough season of life, or shows up for coffee with open ears and supportive, compassionate words. In my own seasons of grief, a timely hug or a supportive word has been the best "medicine" anyone could have prescribed.

We need the comfort and care of others at every age and not only for our emotional well-being, but for our physical health as well. In his work on the medical consequences of loneliness, Dr. James J. Lynch points out that, despite all of our advancements and expenditures in health care, one of our biggest health concerns in industrialized countries is the decline of connection and communication. His research shows a direct correlation between loneliness and cardiovascular problems, such as hypertension and issues with blood pressure. He concludes "... (there are) links between social isolation and increased incidence of premature death in adulthood."[8] When our relationships include positive physical touch, there may be additional health benefits as well, such as improved mood and even alleviation of some types of physical pain.

Perhaps the greatest example of the healing power of relationships comes from the Twelve Step community. In 180 countries worldwide, around 123,000 Alcoholics Anonymous groups regularly meet to provide structure, compassion, and hope for the estimated two million participants who struggle with the disease of alcoholism. Chapter Two of the *Big Book of AA* titled "There Is a Solution," describes the importance of a community like this: "We are people who normally would not mix. But there exists among us a fellowship, a friendliness, and an understanding which is indescribably wonderful."[9] This same type of healing community exists in groups that meet to support its participants through grief, cancer, suicide, mental illness, trauma and many other struggles. (See Resources at the end of the book for more info.)

4. Relationships provide opportunity to love others.

Being in a relationship with others gives us an opportunity to love them. Yes, you read that correctly! By extending ourselves to focus on the needs of someone else (in a healthy way), we do ourselves a favor in the long run.

It might be a stretch to say that I am allowing Mary to enjoy the benefits of being a loving person by being friends with her. But there is some truth to that statement. When I allow her to care for me and I receive her gift of love and friendship, it is also good for her soul. And when I get to reciprocate by supporting her, laughing and sharing, we form a bond that gives us both strength and courage.

I would propose that this is especially true for those of us who profess to follow Jesus. His mandate to love others was very clear and he demonstrated sacrificial love throughout his life. In his book *Loving People*, psychologist Dr. John Townsend - also an expert on boundaries, we will hear more about him later - challenges the belief that authentic love is draining. Instead, he proposes that when we pour into others, we develop a skill (I would call it a relational muscle) that will help both the giver and the receiver.[10]

Here are a few of the benefits he lists for people who practice loving others:

- improved and strengthened relationships in general

- capacity for greater intimacy

- fewer feelings of guilt or fear

- more authenticity

- improved quality of life

- greater personal success

- improved leadership ability

- increased spiritual connection

It is important to note that loving others does NOT mean that I sacrifice my health, my serenity, or my values for someone else. But it CAN lead to temporary discomfort if I choose to give of my time or resources. My neighbor who babysits her grandkids with great gusto and consistency does so because she loves her "littles" and wants to support her kids. Yes, she feels tired, but when they leave, she is also grateful and happy. Contrast her experience to that of a different neighbor who feels obligated to play "dog-nanny" for her son's new puppy. Although she has a demanding job and would prefer to be enjoying some down time on the sofa in the evening, she agrees when he asks for help because she feels guilty saying no. Her resentment is palpable every time she opens the door to greet her fluffy canine guest.

A Faith Perspective

Our **sense of self**, our continued **development** and spiritual **growth**, and our personal and collective **healing** depend on our ability to allow the company and care of others to help us flourish. And it would follow that a healthy relationship, *rooted in love*, is one that supports those things in both parties. From a Christian viewpoint, this kind of love is recognizable in the way we treat each other. The apostle Paul says it this way:

"Love is patient and kind; love does not envy or boast; it is not arrogant or rude. It does not insist on its own way; it is not irritable or resentful; it does not rejoice at wrongdoing, but rejoices with the truth." (1 Corinthians 13:4-6, ESV)

Notice that Paul never puts a qualifier on *who* is deserving of our love. We are called to behave lovingly toward *everyone* as an extension of the love we receive from God. Even when it feels justified, raging against people I dislike or lashing out at those I disagree with does nothing to promote healing or change. When I find myself reacting out of anger and hurt, it is my job to take a deep breath, push "pause" on my actions and examine the roots of my feelings.

At the same time, having a loving disposition is not an invitation to allow others to hurt us or take advantage of our "good nature." Being kind, humble and honest are not the same thing as being passive, submissive or humiliated. (We will talk about this more in the chapters to come.)

Putting it all Together

Let's talk about these concepts as they apply to your own life. If you sense you have "gone missing," want to reclaim your serenity, and want to have healthier relationships, there are two very important things to think about:

1. You need stable, healthy people in your life.

These are people who will support you, speak the truth to you and show up for you when you need them. Strange as it might sound, if you are in a relationship that is difficult, you need to enlist the help of "non-difficult" friends to help you move forward. This type of friend might be your 92-year-old grandmother, the receptionist at work, an old college roommate, the music director from church, or your gym partner. Educational background, vocation, or financial status are not important here. Trust, love, mutual respect, shared values and honesty are.

We should also consider that different levels of friendship can serve different purposes. Closest to you is your inner circle - a few trusted people you can call upon for support (see diagram below). A pastor at my church calls this your "board of directors" - they have permission to speak truth to you and have a vested interest in seeing you succeed. You have vetted them and invited them onto your board and they have accepted the invitation. Further out from the core are close friends, many of whom you interact with through work, recovery, hobbies, or a shared history. The last layer is friends or acquaintances you connect with occasionally. These may be people who were once very important during a different season of life and you currently don't want or need to pull them closer.

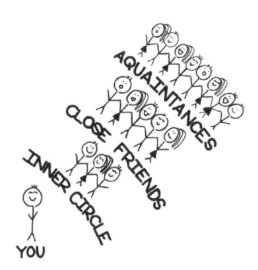

I make it a regular exercise to revisit and even re-work my circles to include someone new or sometimes to prune a friend (gently) who is no longer close. You might cringe at the thought of relegating anyone out of the circle, but I see it as an important part of self-care. As hard as I try to deny it, I have limited time and resources and I want to avoid over committing and over promising. Naturally, I don't make an official announcement as I do this.

While organizing and re-organizing our "people" may be daunting for some of us, one confession I often hear from clients is that they can't think of even *one person* to populate their inner circle. Circumstances and life-events have left them feeling isolated and void of real friends - the kind you can speak to candidly and lean on for support. In addition, they sometimes feel a sense of defeat looking at everyone else's "perfect life" on social media.

There is no shame in admitting that making friends and keeping relationships intact can be hard! Some people are better at it than others. There are many ways to go about connecting or re-connecting with other humans, but my suggestion is to approach this task by focusing on one person at a time. The questions at the end of this chapter might be helpful in this undertaking. Or peruse the list of ideas under "Further Resources" at the end of the chapter.

2. You need to decide what healthy and unhealthy relationships look like for you.

Despite what you may have learned growing up, you are not required to tolerate anyone you dislike. Savor that thought for just a moment and remember you are ridiculously in charge of yourself. You get to choose whom you pull close and whom you don't. Even when family expectations and traditions dictate otherwise, you do not need to invite your Aunt Mabel to your home and you can absolutely continue dating your boyfriend Rick, even if your father disapproves of him. Of course, there might be consequences for severing or engaging in a particular relationship, but the point is you get to weigh the options and chose.

The first task before you is to decide whether the people you surround yourself with are healthy and life-giving. Do they show you unconditional love and support in good and in difficult times? Do they uphold your values, affirm you, and give you the feeling that you matter? (We will talk more about your values and needs in Chapter Five.) The second task is just the first task in reverse: Who drains you? Who pushes your buttons or causes you to become defensive, hostile, or even ashamed? Who causes you to walk on eggshells? At this stage, you do not need to decide whether to end a relationship that falls into this category. The goal is just to become ruthlessly honest and aware.

In the next chapter, we will take what we have learned about healthy connection to evaluate the relationships that make us unhappy or cause us pain.

Reflection Questions:

1. Think about a person you enjoy being in a relationship with.

   - What do you like about him/her?

   - How do you feel when you are in his/her presence?

2. Recall a time when you were hurting, grieving, or just unhappy.

   - Were other people able to help?

   - If so, how? If not, what would you have needed?

3. Think about a time when you intentionally showed love to another person.

- What did you do?

- What effect did it have on the other person?

- How did you feel?

4. Create your own "levels of friendship" diagram.

- What do you notice as you do this exercise?

Further resources:

CHAPTER 2

Dependence and Codependence

"I'm sticking with you cause I'm made out of glue." - *The Velvet Underground*

There is a scene in the movie *Jerry Maguire* that always makes me cringe.[11] It's actually a phrase that a desperate Jerry (Tom Cruise) blurts out as he is attempting to reconcile with his estranged wife Dorothy (Renée Zellweger). Feeling remorseful and lonely, Jerry strides into his sister-in-law's living room (interrupting a lively all-female book club), and sweetly declares his love in a tender and vulnerable way. But then he ends his profession with three disappointing words:

"You complete me!"

Ugh. No, Jerry, no! We can tell you miss her and the sentiment is beautiful (seriously, who wouldn't want to be on the receiving end of a love proclamation like that one?). But those words should send up a host of red flags for your beloved. "Wait, I *complete* you?

Whoa, that's a lot of pressure! What parts of you are missing? Will there be more holes to fill in the future? Does that mean you have to complete me too?"

Go ahead, hate me for ruining one of your favorite movie moments. Obviously, I know nothing about writing a successful Hollywood blockbuster. In my script, Jerry would have confessed, "I don't understand why I struggle with commitment, Dorothy, but please be patient with me. I am working really hard with my therapist to figure out how to lay new neural pathways." It would leave the audience scratching their heads instead of drying their tears.   My point is that overly depending on someone else for our happiness, for our well-being or our joy, can take us down a slippery slope headed for disappointment and instability, and when we gather momentum, we might struggle to stop. Sometimes our desire to turn someone into the person we need them to be can make us behave in ways that are unkind, unhelpful, and overwhelming. And when we spend too much of our time and energy on trying to control someone else's life, we often end up neglecting our own.

The Right Balance

Relationship magic happens when two healthy people come together as authentic and whole (albeit imperfect) human beings who already know who they are, what they value and how to get their needs met. We call this connection ***interdependent*** (see diagram) a place where we are confident of each other's intentions and where honesty and trust go hand in hand with occasional sacrifice and support. As a sidenote, this kind of self-awareness is part of a lifelong journey and not something we just figure out once and for all.

When we are interdependent, we can certainly complement each other with our personalities or encourage and advocate on each other's behalf. But the work of becoming "complete" is our own responsibility.

When a relationship becomes something unsafe or no longer desirable, we can choose to be **independent** from each other (see diagram). It is perfectly legitimate to temporarily (or indefinitely) put some physical or emotional distance between ourselves and someone who causes more harm than good.

As we touched on in the previous chapter, the downside of becoming too independent with too many people is that we miss out on the relational "goodies" like love, support, and affirmation.

Unhealthy Dependence

Fixing, controlling or attempting to change someone are strategies that fall into a relationship category called **codependence**. Maybe you have heard that term before, or maybe you have even called yourself or someone else a "codependent." The word has definitely taken a hit over the last few years - often used as a label for anyone who has tried to give advice or help someone who is struggling. I have listened to shame-filled people say things like, "I am so codependent on him," or ask, "Is it OK to give her money or is that being a codependent?" Let's give the word a proper definition and then look at a few examples.

My favorite description of a codependent person comes from Melody Beattie, author of the groundbreaking book *Codependent No More*: ***A person who has let another person's behavior affect him or her and who is obsessed with controlling that person's behavior.***[12] Read that one more time and notice that there are two parts of that statement. The first part claims that *a codependent person lets someone else's behavior affect them*. Well, I'm going to venture a guess someone else's behavior has affected 100 percent of us. It's part of being human, right? If my spouse is continually rude to my favorite barista or my sister announces she is getting divorced, I am guaranteed to have some emotional reaction or at least sense a rush of adrenaline. But the second part of the definition is where codependency takes shape: we have an *obsession with wanting to control (stop, fix, change) that behavior*. Scheming up ways to get back at my barista-offending hubby or sitting up at night wondering if I could have prevented my sister's divorce are two examples of this kind of behavior.

As the diagram shows, a **codependent** relationship is one of imbalance. If I become so focused on solving your problems or changing your behavior, in some way I get "swallowed up." In this space, I can no longer operate with confidence or freedom because my primary focus is on regulating you.

CODEPENDENT

Who Me?

Admittedly, when I first learned about codependency it was shocking to me. I literally had to sit down and reflect on what I was hearing. I was definitely a "fixer." Not in the physical sense. I could not change a tire to save my life or build a deck that would support more than a chipmunk. But I was pretty convinced I could change people's thoughts, attitudes and feelings. And I believed I had an obligation to do so! After all, my kids needed lessons on how to be wonderful family members, my husband needed to learn how to empty the dishwasher properly and my mom needed support in managing her disrespectful husband. I was there to help people improve, and I saw no harm in that. Was it obsessive? I definitely did not sit in a corner wringing my hands and chanting "woe is me." But it got me wondering where my thoughts go all day - when I am driving, making dinner, at work, etc. It was a sobering moment.

Expert Confessions

I want to share two examples from the highlight reel of my most glaring codependent behaviors just to let you peek behind the curtain of the master. I'm great at it and I learned from the best.

Story 1: I have four amazing, lovable brothers. One of them in particular has a gregarious, larger-than-life personality. I expect to hear his laughter the moment I arrive at his house. His general disposition is a cross between "that sounds dangerous, let's try it" and "don't ask in advance, we can always apologize later." He is my go-to person for financial advice, tour guide for family vacations and lay-therapist when the going gets rough. But, this bundle of energy and can-do spirit also has an Achilles heel: his temper.

When things do not go his way (which they often do not) and when people do not live up to his standards (which they often do not), his automatic response is to ramp up, push back and get heated. In some mysterious sibling way, I can sense the eruption coming simply by reading the tension in his jaw and the stress lines around his eyes. Sometimes, when he and I are in the same room, I become so attuned to understanding his mood that I mentally check out of a conversation I am having with someone else. I will slink over into his vicinity, ready to round out the edges of any conversation that has the potential to lead to the slightest provocation. His temper makes me so uncomfortable that I will do just about anything to prevent it from coming alive.

Do I fit the definition of a codependent when I am around my brother? His behavior definitely affects me. But am I obsessed with wanting to control him? Let's look at it from another angle. What would I be doing in that situation if he had not been in the room? Chatting, eating, relaxing and having fun, right? But instead, the moment he walks in, I automatically shift my attention to managing his mood. Going back to the diagram, I pivot toward him and allow myself to get lost in his thoughts and behaviors. If I think about it, I have been doing this for a really long time. He was two (and I was eight) when he developed his cute "angry voice" so it has been almost fifty years. I think we can call half a century an obsession.

I want to pause here for a moment because I suspect that some of you might be unsettled about that example. In my workshops, I often get a question at this stage that sounds something like this: *But what else are you supposed to do when someone you are close to acts like a jerk? Are you just supposed to ignore it and pretend it isn't happening?* When I call any behavior into question - even though I always start with my own - people naturally get defensive. In fact, you might feel irritated with me right now and that is perfectly normal. The purpose of this chapter is not to place judgment or even to solve a particular relational problem. It is simply to notice that in many subtle and not-so-subtle ways, we might have a propensity to get overly focused on someone else's "business" and when we get too involved with trying to manage that person, we sometimes pay a price for it.

Story 2: The relationship dynamic I described between my little brother and me has all but disappeared. To his credit, he has worked hard to learn to manage his temper, and I have worked equally hard to quit my obsession with fixing him. But in the relationship with my spouse, the stakes were higher and codependent behaviors more pronounced. You met him briefly in the introduction, when I shared about hitting my rock bottom in the wake of his addiction to alcohol. It was a wicked time, to be sure. Anyone who has lived with an alcoholic spouse or family member could write their own book about the scars that the disease inflicts on everyone it involves. But there was more to my spouse than his addiction - Rainer was a man in great emotional pain that struggled with an illness he did not ask for as well as a history of trauma, shame and neglect.

He was a jovial, optimistic, and good-natured person who had many redeeming qualities. His friends and family would describe him as gracious, kind, and self-sacrificing. But one behavior that used to drive me nuts about Rainer was his propensity to say inappropriate things in public, especially when he was drinking. He loved to be provocative, and I am confident he also enjoyed getting a rise out of me. I need to go back just a step and tell you he came from a small, industrial town in Germany, and when I met him, his command of the English language was basic, at best. In fact, most of his vocabulary came from the lyrics printed on the record sleeves of the albums he bought from various US and UK artists. He would often say adorable things like, "Hang on honey, I have to check my look in the mirror" (Bruce Springsteen) or "I was out of that meeting like a bat out of hell" (Meatloaf).

After marrying an American (me) and studying and working in the US for several years, his English improved dramatically, which enabled him to express himself much better (and often in poor taste - at least in my book). He was never terribly profane, but just sexually inappropriate enough to make me uncomfortable. And he got away with it in public because he would grin and twinkle his eyes and say, "I can't help it, I'm European." I couldn't stand it, and despite repeated efforts to get him to stop, he would not.

Confronted with that kind of behavior today, I would simply remove myself from it. Not as a punishment, but as a boundary around the things I will not tolerate. But back then, I did not know that was an option. And I believed his jokes would leave people with the wrong impression of *me* and so I tried to stop him. I begged him to quit, but he would not and as a result, I resorted to rolling my eyes, giving him the cold-shoulder, making excuses for him or trying to change the subject before he could unleash another joke. In fact, our friends knew for certain that there would come a time in any evening that he would say something so outlandish I would elbow him and proclaim in mock disbelief, "Rye Ner"! To everyone else it was funny, but to me it was not. I was ashamed of myself in those situations and it frustrated me I could not get him to change.

The Things We Do

To be clear, I was not the victim in this dynamic. My codependent behaviors were unkind and disrespectful, even if I thought they had merit. But how do we decide when a relationship has become codependent? Interestingly, the answer does not lie in the behavior of the other person. It lies in our own actions and reactions. The Recovery Village lists the most common codependent characteristics as:

1. Covering for another person's shortcomings

When someone else is "messing up" and we repeatedly intervene and save them, or save the day.

2. Being worried that the other person will leave

When we hold back from doing the right thing or telling the truth for fear that the other person might sever the relationship.

3. Focusing on the other person's emotions

When we walk on eggshells or act over accommodating in anticipation of someone else's mood.

4. Putting the other person's needs before your own

When we habitually defer to someone else's desires at the expense of our own needs, health, or sanity.

5. Letting go of our personal values for the other person

When we allow behaviors or act ourselves in a way that is incongruent with what we believe is right and wrong.

6. Keeping track of the other person

When we become obsessed with knowing where someone is all the time, often to verify someone else's poor choices or prevent someone else from making them.

7. Attempting to convince others of the right way to do things

When we give unsolicited advice or information to someone who has not asked for it or does not want to listen to it.

8. Avoiding conflict

When we back down, struggle to stand up for ourselves or turn a blind eye to issues for fear of an altercation, withdrawal, or other forms of relational punishment.

9. Self-Harm

When we become physically or mentally ill or engage in risky or harmful behaviors to cope with the stress or pain of being in a particular relationship.[13]

Are any of those behaviors familiar to you? During the workshop, I often hear groans (and a little laughter) as we go through each of these tendencies, with more groans (and laughter) when we ask everyone to name their top offense. We all engage in these behaviors from time to time and the goal is to recognize when we are doing these things and to take steps toward doing something different to restore our sense of peace. Ownership of our own behaviors is paramount to this process.

Advanced Tactics

Codependents are a sophisticated bunch. As we go about our business, we can be clever, tactical, and even dramatic. We are known to beg, yell, turn a cold-shoulder, throw a tantrum, scold, shame, lecture, weep, withhold love, withhold sex, offer more sex, lie, say "yes" when we mean "no", "no" when we mean "yes" and the list goes on. We think we are justified in trying anything to get someone to behave the way we want them to, but before we get too self-righteous, we have to ask ourselves this very important question:

Is it Working?

Are these strategies or techniques really going to restore our serenity or bring about long-lasting relational change? Or are they more of a temporary fix to give us some illusion of control?

If you can stand it, please ask yourself one last question: *How do you feel when someone tries to fix, change or control you?* Irritated, angry, deflated and ashamed are some answers I usually get when I ask this question of my clients. Definitely not "loved and cared for" or "motivated to change." In my experience, people do not change because someone points out the error or their ways, offers them the perfect logical argument, or withholds affection long enough to show them what they are missing. People change when they want to. When they are ready, willing, or in enough pain that they are interested in doing something new or different. In the chapters to come, we will focus on the only person we can change: ourselves.

No Laughing Matter

Let's come up for air for just a second before we do one more deep-dive. So far in this chapter, we have learned that codependent behaviors and obsessive thoughts are not good for us or for the person on the receiving end. We have admitted to trying our hand at *some* of these practices in *some* relationship. No judgment. Even after years of working on minding my business and letting go of control, I still slip up from time to time and now I can laugh about it, make amends and move on.

In fact, in some ways, we might even find codependent relationships slightly endearing; I mean, interactions between overbearing mamas and their eye-rolling teenagers are sometimes quite funny. My favorite offender is Marie Barone from the hilarious TV sitcom Everybody Loves Raymond.[14] Completely convinced that her loved ones desperately need her guidance, Marie defends her position as matriarch of the family by force feeding those around her a steady diet of relational manipulation disguised as help, concern and love. Too afraid to confront her out-of-control behavior, her family willingly obliges creating one comedic encounter after the next.

But at the risk of sounding overly dramatic, I would also like to point out that codependency has a darker side to it that comes with serious consequences. When we spend too much of our time and energy wrapped up in patterns of obsessive thoughts and when we become "hooked on" fixing, changing and controlling someone, our physical and emotional health can be at risk. The same advances in neuroscience that validate the importance of relationships in our continued development also are helping us see what happens to our brains when those relationships run afoul.

For example, one of the major issues for those of us who struggle with codependency is chronic anxiety brought on by feelings of helplessness and hopelessness. The stress that results from obsessive thoughts and worries can affect our brains in much the same way that obsessive-compulsive disorders and Post-Traumatic Stress Disorders do. Researchers have found that the chemicals released with constant stress can produce a wide range of negative effects on the brain, ranging from mental illness to actually shrinking the volume of the brain.[15] These findings show that prolonged stress can change brain structure, kill off brain cells and impede memory. Those of us who have suffered a season of profound grief often share a common experience of "brain fog" marked by difficulty in decision-making and a general sense of forgetfulness.

A Burdened Wife

Amy and I began a coaching relationship because she felt completely overwhelmed. And she was not kidding. During our first session, she could barely make eye contact with me and her body looked oddly frozen as she recounted the stress in her life. Between deep breaths, she confessed that her husband of many years was involved in yet another affair and she was not sure what to do. While her life, her hopes and dreams were unraveling, she continued to live side by side in the same house as him, and she described being unable to make any decisions at all. Amy felt an obligation to continue to cook, clean and care for him because, in her words, "he is the breadwinner of the family and I don't really do anything to contribute." While confident that his behavior was wrong, she still made excuses for him and blamed herself for his infidelity, at one point telling me she must not be attractive or smart or fun enough for him. She had told no one about his years of philandering for fear that it might ruin his reputation. When we tried to consider the options she had before her, she wept and held her head in utter confusion.

Amy's codependent tendencies were linked to years of marital abuse, as assessed by a licensed therapist. But even as laypersons, we can look at her actions and spot some of how her own behaviors were harming her. And yes, you read that correctly. While her husband was the one who stepped outside of their marriage with great impunity, Amy was actively taking part in her dilemma by making excuses for him, covering for his shortcomings and letting go of her own values. When she confronted him and he blew up at her, she withdrew and became more and more isolated and confused. The constant stress of her marriage was taking a toll on her health, and her quality of life seemed to diminish. Clearly, she and her hopes and dreams had gone missing.

In time, and with tremendous courage, Amy recovered. (We will talk more about the path to recovery and the tools to combat codependency in the second half of the book.) She continued to get professional help and after several months, she could weigh her options realistically and set boundaries to protect what was important to her. Her lovely smile and sense of humor reemerged. It was not a straightforward journey, but one that she would readily admit was well worth it.

In the next chapter, we will consider what we learned about relationships in our formative years and how untreated trauma may be contributing toward our codependent behaviors.

Reflection Questions:

1. Think about a relationship you are in that is difficult.

   • Describe why it is difficult.

   • List some ways you have tried to manage these difficulties.

   • Are you obsessed with trying to control, fix, or change the other person? If so, how?

2. Which of the nine characteristics of codependents listed under "The Things We Do" resonated with you? Which tactics have you employed?

3. Do you notice your own health or wellbeing eroding in a particular relationship? If so, in what way?

4. Do you ever feel that you have "gone missing" in a relationship? If so, how did it happen?

Further resources:

CHaPTer 3
Templates and Trauma

"I do not understand what I do. For what I want to do, I do not do, but what I hate I do." - *Romans 7:15.*

So far, we have established that humans need other people to survive and to thrive. As we mature and develop our character within the confines of different relationships, sometimes things can get imbalanced. We might rely too much on someone for our happiness or become involved in their problems to a point that it is no longer good for us. Our work is to find a way out of the imbalance, out of the codependency we described in the previous chapter. But before we head that direction (and because self-awareness is so crucial to this journey), it behooves us to reflect on *why* we get caught up in unhealthy patterns. Why do we allow ourselves to become so dependent on the feelings and actions of other people? Why do we cringe when we disappoint someone or why do we resist doing something that would be good for us just because someone else may not like it?

We often find the answers in the past.

Looking Back

Digging around in our past can be hard. I will be the first to admit it. There are things I prefer not to talk about, people I don't care to remember, and situations I would rather not have to experience again. I have sat with many clients who were frustratingly stuck in patterns of behavior that bore the scent of their upbringing, but were afraid to take a look back. People who dismiss or avoid therapy often claim that "the past is the past" and there is nothing we can do to change that now. Others will stoically proclaim that blaming our parents is a cop-out and that faith, strength and determination are all we need to claim our own destiny. Some of us are unwilling to poke holes into a family narrative that has been upheld for years in fear that it might upset others.

I totally get it. In fact, you may reflect on a wonderful childhood filled with nurturing adults who challenged, supported, and loved you well. Or you may recall that things were fairly "normal" until an event like divorce or death occurred. Certainly, some of us remember something else: adults who were absent, who struggled with an addiction or mental illness, or were physically or emotionally abusive. No two experiences are the same and subsequently, we will not find the path to a healthier life in a one-size-fits-all solution.

But as we move forward, perhaps we can agree on two things:

- The choice to revisit all or some of your past (with or without professional guidance) is entirely up to you.

- The goal of this work is NOT, and I cannot say this emphatically enough, to blame others or place responsibility for our current behaviors on someone else's shoulders. It is simply to understand why we are the way we are so that we can heal and move forward into a hope-filled future.

A Supportive Sibling

Let's see how you would respond in the following situation. You have an adult brother who is really struggling. He got fired from another job, lost his license to a DWI, and is on the verge of losing his wife and kids as well. You agree to let him stay in your guest room until he gets his life back in order, and you do the best you can for him, including cooking meals and doing laundry. Eight months have gone by, and you are wondering about his progress. From what you see, he spends most of his time watching Netflix and playing video games with his high school buddies. He has not offered to help with chores, although he does stack his beer cans neatly on the floor. You have repeatedly offered suggestions about finding work, going to AA, and making strides toward connecting with his kids, to which he responds, "You are right, I should do that." But nothing changes except for your level of irritation, which is rising.

A healthy next step in this situation would be to have a boundary conversation with this out-of-control brother. It might sound like this:

"Hey Tom. This is a difficult time for you, and I love you and want to support you. I have allowed you to stay at my house thinking it would give you some space and time to help you solve your problems. But I never communicated my expectations for living here and that was not smart of me. Here's the thing: you have everything you need to get yourself back on track and you are choosing not to do so. It is certainly your prerogative to stay unemployed but having you hanging around my home is disrupting my life and adding extra financial and emotional stress. I will allow you to live here for one more month. During that time, I expect you to put your dishes in the dishwasher every night and deal with your own laundry. If you choose not to, you will need to leave immediately."

Typically, when I share a conversation like that with a group, there is one overwhelming response: "No way! I could never say that or follow through. He is my brother." And then a litany of reasons follows:

- I would feel guilty kicking him out to the curb.

- It might devastate his kids.

- He wouldn't have money for food and might starve.

- In our family, they taught us to help each other out.

- He will never find a job if he does not have a permanent address.

Fair enough. Being consistent with our boundaries is tough and might make us look harsh and uncaring. But consider what just happened in that scenario. Your brother made daily choices to not help himself, to take advantage of you and to allow his world to careen out of control. And by letting him use you as his fallback position, you have become the willing enabler of his behavior.

Why would you do this? Where did this kind of relational imbalance come from, and why is it so hard to say no to the people we care about? As you guessed, one answer might be to look for clues in the past. Perhaps you played the role of the caregiver for your siblings as you were growing up or maybe your family praised you for sacrificing your own needs for the sake of someone else in the family. Possibly, you did not receive unconditional love, so you struggle with self-esteem and standing up for yourself. Or maybe you hate to upset anyone for fear that it may reveal something unpleasant about you.

Relational Templates

A variety of factors influences the way we behave in relationships today, including temperament, culture, religious messaging, birth order, physical, emotional or mental challenges, adverse events, trauma and so on. Some of these are innate characteristics (often referred to as "nature") and some are impressed upon us by other people and circumstances (also called "nurture"). Together, these form a **relational template; a set of unconscious rules or patterns that guide our beliefs about human interaction, especially with things like love, acceptance, and trust.**

You gathered much of the information that forms your relational template in the place where you grew up, with the people who raised you. If you watched your father care for his sick mother, for example, he left you with an impression about parent/child relationships. If you were the youngest child and your older siblings often protected you, that experience has been impressed upon you as well.

Because we typically have no other comparison, these formative experiences are what we consider normal - even those that are unhealthy. When we learn to tiptoe around an aggressive relative or hide our feelings to avoid ridicule, our relational template becomes imprinted with information that can later lead to imbalanced and unhealthy relationships. Here are some examples of the information we might learn:

- **Gender roles.** Jake is told that boys are supposed to be tough, and the men in his family tell him not to cry. Instead, he needs to "man up" and keep going. *He learns it is bad to feel sad.*

- **Romantic relationships**. Macy witnesses her mom constantly trying to "improve" her dad by telling him how to dress better, drive more efficiently, stand up for himself at work and so on. *She learns it is acceptable to impose your will on someone else's.*

- **Faith-based messages.** Kasey is told that a Godly woman is submissive to her husband and allows him to make all the decisions. Shannon hears her grandmother say that divorce is a sin. *They learn it may not be appropriate for a wife to stand up for herself in a marriage.*

- **Cultural norms.** Giovanni lives in a large, "family first" community where advice giving and family gossip are a natural way of life. *He learns other people might be in charge of his life and his decisions.*

- **Conflict resolution**. Weston hears his mom tell the other parents that she plans to pull him from the team if the coach does not start playing him more often. *He learns it is acceptable to talk with others about someone's behavior instead of confronting them directly.*

- **Communication.** Kayla's father is short tempered and snappy when he gets home from work. *She learns to make herself "small" and to tiptoe around someone's moods.*

- **Discipline**. Frankie knows that if he throws a fit, his mom will cave in to his demands and he will get his way. *He learns he has the power to cause someone else to back down from their boundaries.*

The Imprint of Trauma

Although they can lead to relational difficulty, most of the experiences just described are fairly innocuous. As we age, and become exposed to more relationships, we will have to examine our beliefs and behaviors (based on our relational template) and decide how we want to act and what we might want to change. Traumatic experiences, however, can leave a deeper imprint on our relational template - one that is often more difficult to decipher.

You are undoubtedly familiar with *physical trauma* - a broken bone, concussion, major surgery or another bodily malady. The results of trauma are often quite visible. You may, in fact, have some fascinating stories to accompany your scars! But even when the damage is internal, it can usually be located with the help of x-ray, ultrasound and advanced imaging.

Emotional trauma (which we will focus on in this chapter) is not so easily recognizable. It is caused by **any type of experience, at any age, that leaves us feeling overwhelmed and helpless**. The degree to which an event is traumatic will differ from person to person. Being robbed at knife point may be something you recover from in a few days, while someone else might become seriously anxious. Trauma expert Lise LeBlanc explains, " (trauma) is more about the nervous system's ability to regulate stress and integrate emotions than it is about the actual event."[16] While emotional trauma can result from a physical event (such as a car accident), it typically occurs in a relationship with someone who is abusive, neglectful, narcissistic, or some other form of uncaring.

Bringing Light to Trauma

Trauma is a hot topic these days. What began as an attempt to understand the impact of war trauma (PTSD) on soldiers has now developed into a full-blown research effort to pinpoint how and where trauma affects the brain and what we can do to prevent and treat it. Celebrities, professional athletes, politicians, authors and other people of influence are sharing their childhood stories of abuse, neglect and violence to encourage others who might suffer or struggle as well.

A quick Internet search will bring up hundreds of books about trauma as it weaves itself into culture, race, politics, parenting, divorce, grief, mental illness and war. Several of these titles are written for children hoping they might learn to address their grief, regulate their emotions and not blame themselves when something bad happens. While we are relying on neuroscience to teach us, one thing is certain: childhood trauma affects not only our cognitive, emotional and physical development but also our ability to find, enjoy and maintain healthy relationships.

A Little Empathy, Please

Oprah Winfrey and Dr. Bruce Perry wrote an outstanding book about understanding our past trauma called *What Happened to You?* It was one of those books where I nodded and said "yes, amen" aloud repeatedly. Here is an excerpt from the jacket cover:

"(They) explore how what happens to us in early childhood influences the people we become. They challenge us to shift from focusing on "What's wrong with you?" or "Why are you behaving that way?" to "What happened to you?... Many of us experience adversity that has a long-lasting impact on our physical and emotional health. What happens to us in childhood is a powerful predicator of our risk for health problems down the road and offers scientific insights into the patterns of behaviors so many struggle to understand."[17]

I love that approach. As we search to understand what motivates us to repeat certain unwanted or confusing behaviors, we can do so with empathy and kindness, knowing that we are not inherently defective, bad or wrong. Imagine what a difference it could make if we consider "problematic" people in the same way. Instead of labeling someone as a "loser" or a "failure," perhaps we will pause to remember that we do not know what got them to the place where they might be losing and failing. This is not to say we should tolerate unacceptable behavior, but a more empathetic approach to another human's shortcomings might be more useful than any broad-sweeping, categorical rejection.

Recognizing Emotional Trauma

All of us have had unpleasant or uncomfortable things happen to us both as children and as adults, but does that mean we are traumatized? That depends. Sometimes a traumatic event will lead to obvious symptoms of mental or emotional distress such as persistent crying, anxiety, depression, self-harm, emotional outbursts, inability to sleep or eat, suicidal thoughts, substance abuse etc. (If you are experiencing any of these symptoms, I would strongly urge you to seek professional help sooner than later. See the Resources at the end of the book.)

But other times, the symptoms can show up much later and we might not remember the details of what actually happened to us. Our unconscious brain, however, never forgets and typically, at some point, unresolved trauma will "leak" into some area of our lives - often into our relationships. For example, when we consistently latch onto people who hurt us, or we struggle to be intimate or vulnerable, we might be dealing with the after-effects of trauma. In his brilliant work *The Body Keeps the Score,* Dr. Bessel van der Kolk shares this example: "If your heart is still broken because you were assaulted by someone you loved, you are likely to be preoccupied with not getting hurt again and fear opening up to someone new."[18]

Family Secrets

Samantha was four when her beloved father left the family. As far as she can remember, he packed his things and disappeared fairly quickly from the scene. Within weeks, a stranger showed up in the home and Samantha's mother reported that he would be her new father and she was to call him daddy. She and her siblings would get a new last name and a new little sister to play with from time to time. Although her mother never said it aloud, Samantha clearly understood that all would be well, provided that everyone kept the family secret and spoke about it no more. As the years passed, and her mother's new marriage fell apart, Samantha became adept at maneuvering around the tensions in the household and staying in good graces by keeping her room tidy, doing well in school, and being compliant. She got used to making herself "unseen" to avoid any kind of trouble.

As she entered adulthood, Samantha found herself full of anxiety. Her lackluster career disappointed her, and a recent "romantic disaster" left her discouraged. When she began thinking of other job options, Samantha realized she knew how she wanted other people to feel about her (hard working, intelligent, diligent), but she had no clue what would actually make her happy. The same was true about dating. She knew how she wanted to be perceived (supportive, kind, intelligent) but she had never considered what *she* actually wanted in a partner. The more she thought about her life and the choices she was making, the more apparent it became that Samantha knew little about her own needs and wants. She was, however, highly attuned to pleasing the people around her.

It would be an oversimplification to say that all of her current struggles could be traced back to the events of her fourth year of life, but trauma could certainly have been at play. Instead of being encouraged to express her sadness at her father's departure, her apprehension toward a new dad, or her confusion about her circumstances, young Samantha was told to keep the peace by keeping secrets, being a good girl and putting on a cheerful face. At a time when she needed to experience the unconditional love and support of the adults around her, she found herself trying to love and support them instead.

On one hand, we can applaud her for learning to cope and adapt in that environment. As a result of her circumstances, Samantha is highly skilled at "reading a room" and understanding what others are feeling and needing. Friends marvel at her ability to listen, comfort and care for them. But we can also recognize that these skills do not always serve her best interests. She unconsciously gauges her self-worth on her ability to make other people happy. Her insatiable desire for outside approval has often left her feeling anxious, rejected and defeated. In many ways, the "authentic" Samantha has been missing since childhood and now, as an adult, she would have to embark on the difficult journey of finding out who she actually was.

The Gremlin of Shame

Before doing the hard work of exploring her past and understanding her emotional and relational deficits, Samantha had a significant hurdle to overcome: she was filled with shame. Tragically, at some point in her life, this likable, intelligent woman believed that she was not only responsible for her struggles, but that *she might actually be a deficient human being* as well. If she was truly going to open up and talk about her past, she might risk exposing this horrible "fact" to someone else. And if she did, she might find out that it was actually true.

Of all of our human emotions, shame is often the most difficult to understand and the most difficult to feel. In his groundbreaking book *The Soul of Shame*, researcher and professor Curt Thompson observes that **shame begins with the notion that "I am not enough- there is something inherently wrong with me."**[19] Popular author and shame researcher Brené Brown says that "shame is the warm feeling that washes over us, making us feel small, flawed, and never good enough."[20] But more profoundly, shame is often accompanied by the sense that "I do not have what it takes to tolerate the feeling of it". If I am laden with shame, I cannot even risk allowing myself to feel it because it is unbearable. Instead, I will do everything in my power to deny it or try to make it go away (which might include having a drink, taking a pill or numbing myself with anything to get rid of it).

It makes sense if you think about how the body does this with physical pain. If the dentist does not give you the correct dosage of novocaine and you start to feel the nauseating burn of the drill, chances are you cannot calm yourself down by thinking, "It will be fine. I can endure this." Most likely, some impulse will catapult you from your chair or you will pass out, which is an equally non-elective reaction. Similarly, when we feel ashamed, our unconscious brain can often take control and convince us that we cannot risk allowing the thoughts behind the emotion, or the emotion itself, to exist. When shame is present, we feel the need to get out, get going, and get away from it as quickly as possible.

Coping but Not Healing

Let me offer you one last example of how past trauma, coupled with shame, can lead to imbalanced, codependent relationships.

Rainer, the husband I introduced you to in the previous chapters, was the son of an alcoholic mother and an emotionally absent father. Like many children raised with active addiction, he was led to sacrifice much of his own childhood to self-protect and manage the adult dysfunction in his home. He took on a pseudo care-taker and mediator role and spent a great deal of time caring for his mom, doing her chores, and running interference when his father verbally reprimanded her. Rainer was also molested by a member of the clergy when he was a teenager. As is common for victims of sexual abuse, he remained silent about it most of his life, until he was in his mid-fifties, struggling with addiction and depression - his life spiraling out of control. Even then, he only ever told one person, and that one person later told me. Clearly the adults who neglected and hurt him had marred his relational template and unfortunately, he carried the imprint of their actions into his adult life, never cognitively understanding how his past would skew his future relationships.

Although he never used the word "shame," Rainer could tell you he always felt profoundly unworthy, unlikeable, and not good enough. He had, however, discovered that he could outmaneuver his feelings of inadequacy by being nice, a skill he was very good at. Outwardly, he was the kindest, warmest person you would ever meet, and in a genuine sense, he lived to make people happy. He loved bringing flowers, buying someone's favorite beer or surprising a family member with suite-level baseball tickets. His hugs were big and generous and often accentuated with a kiss on the cheek. Indeed, everybody loved Rainer and figured his enthusiasm and zest for life were authentic reflections of something solid and joyful in his soul.

But sadly, nothing could have been further from the truth. While he appeared to be coping with his life well, on the inside, he was deeply mired in shame and dependent on others for his self-esteem. When conflict or disapproval showed up at work, he became terribly anxious and worked obscene hours to prove he was worthy. His absence from home made him feel excluded and rejected by the family he loved and wanted to please. Lacking resilience and boundaries, Rainer continued to "put out fires" (his favorite words) as best he could and when he could no longer keep up the facade, he turned to alcohol to ease his pain.

There Is Hope

The content of this chapter and the stories I have shared are heavy. Even if you did not connect with any particular narrative, you may still feel the weight of someone else's suffering. Or this topic might have triggered some painful thoughts about your own experience with trauma.

The good news is that we do not have to settle for an unhappy ending! And we do not have to allow our past to dictate our future. Armed with a bit of courage, a few tools and possibly some professional help, we CAN improve our emotional health and heal our relationships as well. And in my experience, God is eager and willing to redeem and restore us when we are willing to surrender to His help and guidance.

In the next chapter, we will consider how improving our emotional intelligence can help us move closer to health and healing.

Reflection Questions:

1. Consider your own relational template.

   • Who were your primary caregivers?

   • What impression were you given about romantic relationships? friendship? gender roles? family?

   • How was conflict handled? How did you communicate together?

   • Which of these patterns do you carry over into your relationships today?

2. Consider your own experience with adversity or trauma.

   • How comfortable do you feel talking with others about your past?

   • Are there relationship patterns you might be perpetuating because of some past event? If so, have you considered speaking with a professional about them? (See additional resources at the end for tips on how to find a therapist.)

3. What reaction did you have to the description of shame and the way it can control us?

4. Can you remember an experience that made you want to hide or disappear? What happened?

Further resources:

CHAPTER 4
Emotional Intelligence

"Today you are You, that is truer than true. There is no one alive who is Youer than You." - *Dr. Seuss.*

The first section of this book laid a foundation for our understanding of positive and negative relational dynamics and the way our past experiences influence the way we behave around others today. In the second part of our journey, we are going to turn our focus toward evaluating our *present* "inner landscape" and learning about tools that help us regulate our emotions, react in positive ways, and let go of things that are out of our control. Armed with this information, we will be ready to consider setting healthy limits to protect what is important to us. If this terrain seems foreign (or even daunting) to you, rest assured we will scale this mountain together, putting one foot in front of the other and keeping our common goal in mind: getting "unstuck" from relationships that are not good for us.

Relax, it will be fun!

A Health Obsession

As a society, we are slightly obsessed with our health. Maybe "obsessed" is too strong a word, but can we at least agree that we place great emphasis on our **physical** appearance and wellbeing? We measure our waistlines, step on scales and check our BMI to get information about how we are doing and where we want to improve. We submit to routine exams to check our cholesterol and blood pressure, to detect cancer and other abnormalities, and to prevent illness and disease. We cycle, run, swim, supplement, diet and hydrate to be in the best shape possible and we aim to live a long (and hopefully) pain-free life. Indeed, US consumers spend $265 billion annually on physical activity - more than any other country in the world and one third of the entire global market.[21]

Like most industrialized nations, we have a similar tendency with our **intellectual** health. We want to know how smart we are and how we can be smarter. We send our kids to summer science camp and sign them up for private tutoring to help them succeed in the classroom and give them an advantage in life. We gauge their intelligence by comparing IQs, GPAs, ACT and SAT scores, as well as National Merit and Presidential honors. We reward our little Einsteins with cash for straight A's and take away their media time when they perform poorly. We give awards to those who excel in their fields and list our accolades and degrees on our social and professional media profiles. We encourage creative solutions, thinking outside the box, and breakthroughs that lead us to understand and manage our world better.

Mind you, there is nothing inherently wrong with any of these pursuits. Honoring and protecting our bodies and living in our full cognitive potential is something most of us would endorse (and some of us occasionally get around to doing). But only recently have we begun to investigate another crucial landscape: our **emotional and mental health**. Compared to our fixation with our bodies and our intellect, many of us come into adulthood knowing shockingly little about **our thought processes, our feelings, and our fundamental beliefs and values.** We often wish we could be more assertive in a conflict situation, but we are afraid of the repercussions. Some of us struggle to "turn off" the intrusive thoughts in our head. And others of us think everything is "under control" only to one day find out it is not.

The Trip that Never Happened

I had my first panic attack standing on a sidewalk in Canterbury, England when I was twenty years old. I had no idea what was happening to me and although I couldn't fathom the idea of a person my age having a heart attack, it seemed like the only logical explanation. Prior to that day, I had been preparing to take a trip to visit my good buddy who was attending the University of Brighton, while at the same time, I was studying in Germany. I planned to first spend a week alone traipsing through a few cities south of London, and then take a train to Brighton to hang out with my friend. Eventually, we wanted to join another classmate and backpack for two additional weeks through Italy and Greece. I had activated my train pass and filled my backpack with three types of foreign currency, travel sized cosmetics, 35 mm film, and a blank journal. It was going to be an epic trip that we would talk about for years to come.

After a grueling twenty-four-hour drive across the countryside of France (in a loud 1960s VW Beetle), and a ferry ride over the English Channel, I finally stood alone in front of a dingy Canterbury youth hostel. Exhausted but still excited, I was admiring this picturesque medieval town when I noticed my chest slowly tightened. Over the next few minutes, the sensation became more acute and spread to my abdomen, my back, and my throat. I worried I might pass out and cause a scene or worse, I might actually die. My heart raced, the color drained from my face, and I noticed a wave of salty, hot tears dripping from my eyes.

I wish I had known at the time that the feeling taking over my body was not a heart attack but a wave of chemicals and impulses being sent by my brain to communicate something important. Although I had convinced myself that this solo adventure was going to be exciting, a "hidden part" of my brain did not approve. And it was trying to get my attention.

But at that time in my life, I didn't know that my brain had anything to do with my emotions, or that it might want to communicate with me. As far as I was concerned, my feelings came from my heart. I somehow believed that the organ pumping blood through my body, keeping my cells alive, was also responsible for my happiness, fear, and sadness. Don't laugh! I'm guessing you were sold a similar bill of goods. Did anyone ever call you a "heart breaker" or claim that you were "breaking their heart"? Can you count the number of love songs written about hearts that must go on, hearts that ache (in an achy, breaky way) or hearts that will never mend? It's ironic, isn't it, that we hold this fist-sized muscle in our chest cavity responsible for our pain and sorrow when it is our brain that is actually the culprit.

What happened next was a whirlwind, and to this day I am still unsure of all the details. Somehow I found a train to Brighton that night, and I ran like an Olympian across the university campus trying to locate my American friend. Unable to calm my body down, I flew back to Germany two days later and then headed back to Los Angeles the day after that. Exhausted from crying and still enveloped in anxiety, I was utterly disappointed that my dream trip would not transpire. It was good to see my mom at the airport and I had hoped my problems would have disappeared by the time I landed on the Pacific Coast. But unfortunately, I could not outrun or out fly them.

Engaging a counselor or talking about anxiety was not the norm in the 1980s, but my mom was friends with a therapist so, out of desperation for both of us, she sent me to see him. I remember those visits vividly as they marked the start of the most meaningful journey of my life; more important than the travel adventure I was missing out on. Seated nervously on the edge of a stiff leather chair in his overly air-conditioned office, I began to speak to my therapist about what had happened to me. But the words that came out of my mouth sounded like those of a stranger and I started to wonder if I would ever find my "old self" again.

We talked about living abroad, expectations of the trip, and loss of connection to my friends and family. He explained the dynamics of anxiety and that while it was highly uncomfortable it was not necessarily a bad thing. As we continued to explore, I felt validated and understood and within a few hours; we replaced the gripping fear in my chest with calm and peace. I promised myself that in the future, no matter what, I was never, ever going to shut down or ignore another feeling again. Instead, I would a prevent a future "ambush" by learning everything I could about my inner landscape.

I would love to tell you I was successful in keeping anxiety (or panic attacks) at bay for the rest of my life. In truth, I continued to wrestle with both, weeping in school parking lots and sobbing alone in my bed, begging God to fix me. I sat through tough hours of traditional and trauma therapy, tried medication, and practiced meditation and mindfulness. Slowly, over time, healing has come. Even though the work was (and is) hard, I kept the promise I made to my twenty-year-old self to fearlessly continue trudging forward.

We All Bear the Burden

I am thankful that my emotional "breakdown" ended well and without long-term complications and I continue to be grateful for the people who help me learn more about my inner wiring. In recent years, there has been a steady up-tick in mental health awareness and access to professional care has improved as well (although there is still much room for improvement). We now encourage families and schools to talk with our children about mental health and look for signs of emotional distress to provide early intervention. Seeking the help of a therapist or coach has become more normal and is no longer equated with weakness.

But so many people are still silently lost in their mental health struggles and missing out on a flourishing life. Without tools to deal with their emotional pain, they numb or distract themselves with substances and behaviors that can permanently affect their physical and cognitive health. As a society, we all experience the aftermath: increases in suicide, addiction, crime, poverty, homelessness, and so on. We need to continue to breakdown the stigma associated with pursuing mental health to allow ourselves, and the people around us to come out of hiding and heal.

Emotional Intelligence Basics

Our mental and emotional health play a huge role in our pursuit of life-giving relationships. If we are going to create meaningful, positive connections with others, we need to be aware of our thoughts, feelings and behaviors. One of the most important (and practical) ways we can do this is by working on our *emotional intelligence* - sometimes referred to as EQ. The Institute for Social and Emotional Intelligence defines EQ as, **"the ability to be aware of our own emotions, and those of others, and to use that information to manage our behavior and relationships appropriately."**[22] According to psychologist Daniel Goleman, we raise our EQ by working on skills such as:

- self-awareness (knowledge of our feelings, skills, self-confidence)

- empathy (our ability to identify with the feelings of others)

- motivation (what drives us to pursue our goals)

- self-regulation (managing our emotions and responses)

- social ability (connecting, interacting and working with others).

For our purposes, we will focus on the first two as they relate to the journey out of codependency.[23]

A Warm-Up

Let's do a five-minute exercise to get the mental/emotional juices flowing. Think of it as a warm-up for the conversation to follow in the rest of this section. Don't worry your answers won't be graded (and you won't be required to look up any score on a mental health index). But I would encourage you to be honest even if your answer is "I don't know." Here are a few prompts to get you started:

1. Name one positive and one negative emotion you had today (beyond mad, sad, or glad).

2. Name something that happened this past year that you regret.

3. Name three things you value in a friendship.

4. Name one habit you are working on changing and how you plan to achieve success.

5. Name one thing you do for self-care when you are depleted or exhausted.

So, what was that experience like for you? Enjoyable? Stressful? Confusing? Boring?

A Challenge

Here is a second exercise to get you thinking about the effect of EQ in everyday life.

Imagine you just pitched an idea at an important meeting and one of your colleagues abruptly critiques you. What would you do?

- If you have high EQ, your first response would be to be aware of your discomfort and recognize that her comment left you angry, hurt or even slightly humiliated. You then discern that the criticism was likely not a personal attack but a thoughtless response from someone who is stressed and buried under deadlines. Or you might objectively acknowledge her comment and consider its merit, even if her delivery was too direct for your liking. You control your temper (by taking a few deep breaths), thank her for her candid feedback, continue to explain your idea, and decide to let the one-and-done incident go.

- If you have lower EQ, you might be so angry by the criticism that you shut down for the rest of the meeting.

Or, out of frustration, you complain to the room that you worked hard on the presentation and sarcastically ask if she has any better ideas. Later, while the other participants move on to different topics, you think about updating your resume, only sharing ideas electronically in the future, or getting back at the offender at some point. At the end of the meeting, you head straight to another colleague's office to air your grievances.

As you consider which of these responses would most likely be your go-to, keep in mind that you will show higher EQ in some relationships and lower in others. You might be incredibly self-regulated in a business setting with your direct reports, but come completely undone when your spouse comments on your parenting. Telling an unhappy friend that you cannot come over might be second nature to you. But you may lose sleep when your mom complains that you never visit. We can all improve and grow in our quest for serenity and healthy relationships!

Admittedly, this information and content may make your head swim just a little. But becoming more self-aware can be a pleasant experience. In my workshops, EQ exercises elicit a ton of laughter and "ah ha" moments because we recognize that we:

- are human with human frailties.

- continue to make mistakes and often do things out of habit that we swore just five minutes prior never to do again.

- often function on autopilot until something requires attention. In the same way, an emergency appendectomy can force us to become familiar with an appendage we cared very little about in the past, so too can a volatile encounter with our spouse lead us to explore our hidden anger issues.

The Role of Feelings and Empathy

Of the many factors that contribute to EQ, the two most important for our work on relationships are: recognizing feelings and developing empathy.

1. Feelings

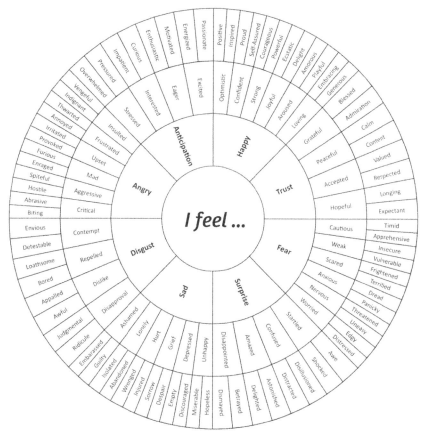

leadskill.com

On this feelings wheel, basic emotions are listed on the inside: happy, fear, angry and so on. As you work your way out from the center, you will see more nuanced feelings of the same root. When you are sad that your NFL team lost the Super Bowl, for example, you might actually be feeling embarrassed about the players you chose for your fantasy team or guilty for having spent so much time obsessing about the season. If you feel angry about being home alone on a Friday night, you might actually be frustrated because your friends did not invite you to go out with them. Note: the feelings wheel is not all inclusive -there are literally thousands of "feelings words" in the English language.

Below are a few scenarios to help you become more familiar with your feelings. As you read each one, consider your very first emotion - not the one you think you should be feeling, but the one that actually comes up right away. Then, ask some friends or family members to respond to the same scenarios and see how they react. It might surprise you to discover the differences or similarities in the reactions to the same situations. I took the liberty of adding my own response for you to compare.

- Someone compliments your outfit. (embarrassed)

- Your credit card gets declined at the grocery store. (ashamed)

- You are snowed in for the day and alone. (lonely)

- Your mother-in-law tries to improve your cooking. (irritated)

- You receive flowers from a secret admirer. (guilty)

- You end an hour-long conversation with your partner or significant other. (energized)

- A letter arrives stating that you are to receive an inheritance. (skeptical)

- You are standing on the platform of a zip-line about to head across the rain forest. (daring)

- You remember Thanksgiving is a few months away. (excited)

- Your tire goes flat on the highway. (terrified)

Did you find anything new or surprising in your responses? If so, you are not alone. I have (literally) seen grown men tear up when they use the feelings wheel for the first time. There is something powerful about being able to name an emotion that has confounded you for a lifetime. Does this work frustrate you? Welcome to the club. These words can seem very foreign. One client habitually defaults to the word "upset" for every negative emotion. She giggled when I banned the word from our conversations but she still slips it in on occasion. Did this exercise make you yawn? Fantastic! You will help those around you by honestly communicating how you are doing (and feeling).

Behind the Feelings

Identifying our emotions is far more than a vocabulary exercise, however. Feelings give us important clues about deeper issues tied to our thoughts and beliefs. When you trip over your child's shoes in the hallway (and unleash a variety of curse words), the anger you experience at that moment is likely related to something you believe about kids putting shoes away. Behind your frustration, you may assume that your child does not care about you or that you did not do a great job of raising him. The hurt you sense when your mother-in-law attempts to make you a better cook could be connected to a belief that you are not good enough. You might also suffer a sense of betrayal when your husband does not stick up for you in her presence.

Those of you with some experience with counseling will recognize this work as part of Cognitive Behavioral Therapy (CBT), one of the most common therapeutic modalities. CBT helps us identify faulty beliefs that might keep us stuck in unwanted behavior patterns. It also helps us correct those beliefs with honest, often more compassionate truths. If the shoe-tripping parent in the example above recognizes that self-blame is at play, we might encourage him to assess his parenting skills in a more calm, rational way and implement new strategies to help his kiddo tidy up. Or he might laugh about the incident and recognize that he is a great parent and that family life is often imperfect. The critiqued cook might recognize that her hurt feelings stem from a general sense of inadequacy based on past experiences. With a little help, she might address these issues and come to appreciate her mother-in-law's suggestions instead of balking at them. Or we might encourage her to initiate a gentle but firm conversation with her MIL about withholding her advice.

Just for fun, (or at least out of curiosity), go back to any of the above scenarios where you had a powerful reaction and ask yourself the question: What is the belief behind that emotion? For example, if someone compliments my outfit, I get embarrassed because I believe they must think I am showing off. Or if they decline my card at the grocery store, I am ashamed because I believe that other people in line will see me as incapable of managing my life. (This does not mean I need to change anything, this is just making an observation to improve my EQ.) Taking it a step further, when you feel a powerful emotion during the day, take a moment to identify it (beyond upset or mad) and consider what was really behind it. Ask yourself if that belief is true, honest, or fair. This process will become easier in time and if you notice a repeated self-defeating belief (I am bad, I am unworthy of happiness etc.), enlist the help of a counselor or coach to help you unpack this more.

2. Empathy

Another important component of EQ is empathy. **Empathy is the ability to recognize someone else's feelings and to understand their perspective**. Most of us sense some level of natural empathy for people who are in a situation that is familiar to us or who struggle with something we can relate to. We cheer on Dory as she attempts to find her way back to her family because we know what it is like to be lost. We desperately hope Forrest Gump will outrun the pack of mean classmates because we remember being outnumbered, bullied or alone. Quite naturally we will gravitate toward people who share a similar experience, giving us an immediate, unspoken connection. The number of groups that are formed to support people struggling with addiction, cancer, grief, divorce, trauma, and so on are evidence of this. There is something about being understood that is good for the soul.

The greater our self-awareness, the better we will be at recognizing the feelings and perspective of others. As we grow in our empathetic skills, we also get better at engaging with people whose experiences differ from our own and we become more curious about someone's different or even conflicting viewpoint. Our EQ will grow when we stretch ourselves to understand people we do not agree with or loved ones whose actions or choices we do not support. Showing empathy doesn't mean we are not condoning someone's behavior or agreeing with their view. We can express our concern and love by trying to understand where they are coming from and by holding space for them to air their thoughts and express their feelings.

The Art of Listening

"Holding space" is one of my favorite newer phrases in the English language. When we resist the urge to fix someone (or their issues) and simply allow them to be in our presence in whatever way they need, it is an act of caring and love. This kind of empathetic listening communicates that we are more interested in the concerns of the other person than our own thoughts and opinions. It requires us to focus on the needs and experiences of the other person, not our own desire to be right, validated, or heard.

Active listening involves turning our bodies toward the speaker, making natural eye contact, and removing distractions. While we might ask curious questions to learn more about the speaker's thoughts, we refrain from sharing our own experience or giving advice unless we ask permission to do so. A good listener does not challenge or negate someone's feelings by telling them to calm down or stop over-reacting. The speaker has a right to their story and the way they experienced it. Who are we to tell them otherwise? This can be especially tricky when we harbor strong opinions about what we are hearing. But with practice we can get better at it. We will talk more about empathetic detachment in Chapter Six.

Think about the last time someone listened to you. I mean, the person truly leaned in to what you were saying, affirmed your feelings, and heard you without adding a lot of their own "stuff" to the conversation. Chances are you felt safe, valued, and even unburdened. But now think about a time when you were desperate to process something important and the person you talked to was not empathetic. Perhaps they offered their advice right away or told you that your feelings were wrong or worse, unimportant. Can you remember what that was like?

My Child, I See You

I worked several months with a mother, Jennifer, who was struggling to connect with her adult daughter, Mia. Mia had been seeing a therapist and was unpacking some deeper issues related to her childhood. Lately, Mia had been talking to her mom about some of the difficulty she encountered growing up with a younger brother who was always in trouble. In her daughter's mind, Jennifer had been so focused on the problems of her other child that she rarely had time for Mia. At a young age, Mia learned to be compliant and supportive of her mom to ensure peace in the house. However, she now noticed that in her adult relationships, she would too often allow herself to become overly attuned to the other person's wants and she rarely spoke up for her own needs or desires.

My client wanted desperately to reconnect with her daughter, but Mia's "accusations" offended her. In Jennifer's mind, she had done the best she could under the circumstances and she could not understand why Mia wanted to blame her for her problems. As Jennifer and I talked more, she shared about her feelings of inadequacy and guilt as an exhausted, single mom with a rebellious child. She was always grateful that Mia had been "the amiable one" but was now seeing that perhaps her daughter did not get the love and support she needed.

Jennifer courageously invited Mia to attend a coaching session, during which she asked her daughter to share anything she wanted. She also promised to listen carefully without getting defensive. At the end of our meeting, I asked Jennifer to look at her daughter and tell her what she loved about her. Her first inclination was to thank her for all the ways she had been kind and helpful over the years - things that had made her life as a mom easier. But then she pivoted and began listing Mia's wonderful qualities: compassionate, creative, interesting, energetic and witty. Mia's demeanor changed entirely, and she appeared to be soaking up her mom's affirmation for the first time. It was a beautiful, sacred moment for all of us.

A Word of Warning

Empathy can be a little tricky for those of us struggle with codependency. When we are programmed to want to fix, control or change people, being overly-empathetic can lead us to spend a great deal of time in someone else's brain (understanding their feelings, their perspectives, their needs) and too little time in our own. There is no formula for knowing when we go too far, but constant worry, sleepless nights, and obsessive thoughts are good indicators that we need to redirect. Try this experiment: how do you respond when someone asks, "How are you?" Do you share primarily about yourself, your work, hobbies, dreams, health, etc.? Or do you immediately default to talking about someone else and their difficulties as if they were your own? The answer to this question can give you a lot of clues about your ability to differentiate between healthy empathy and unhealthy dependence. You might also observe how others respond when *you* ask them this question.

When something traumatic or even exciting happens to someone we care about, we naturally default to thinking about their experience for a while. But as a general rule our relationships will be healthiest when we care about others and empathize with them in a way that interdependently honors our separate identities and our own unique lives. We will continue to talk about this in the chapters to come.

In the next chapter, we will think about our values, needs, and expectations of others and consider how to proceed in relationships where these are not being met.

Reflection Questions:

1. How would you describe your overall Emotional Intelligence? (Scan the QR code at the end to take an EQ test.)

- What could you do to improve your EQ?

2. Look back at the feelings wheel and decide which feeling (or group of feelings)

- is most desirable to you.

- makes you most uncomfortable.

- you would like to have more/less of.

3. How would you rate yourself as a listener?

- Ask the people in your life to give you feedback and then ask them what makes a good listener.

- Try out this exercise: Ask someone you trust to share something important with you and for one minute, just listen. Then ask the other person do the same and reflect on your experience. Consider doing this again and upping your time to two minutes or even three.

Further resources:

CHAPTER 5

Values and Expectations

"We look up at the same stars and see such different things." -
George R. R. Martin, A Storm of Swords

I once had a sweet neighbor named Terri. Every so often, after the kids got on the bus, we would catch up on the latest subdivision news over a cup of coffee. She would also show me the beautiful upgrades being made to her home. Terri was well into her seventies but had recently received her real estate license, claiming she needed something to keep her occupied until she died. Her house was under constant renovation and she seemed to come to life describing to me the details involved in each project. I adored this strong and vibrant woman who spoke with authority and carried herself with great pragmatism.

On one particular morning, my friend shared with me that she felt slighted by a family member who forgot her birthday. In fact, she said bitterly, if she thought long and hard about it (which she did), this was not the first time this person had ignored her.

"I mean, she called to congratulate me and I think last year she emailed, but would it kill her to actually put a card in the mail?" Terri lamented that day. I looked at her with curiosity, believing she had misspoken. In my book, a phone call on my birthday would have been completely sufficient. I would have appreciated a few personal words per telephone more than a Hallmark greeting card with a generic signature at the end. But Terri did not see it this way. She valued the neatly folded card-stock which she could display on her table and keep for years to come. And she never questioned why anyone else wouldn't.

It might seem silly to you that someone would be so persnickety about how to execute the proper birthday wish. But my point is, we all place value on different things in our relationships and we put expectations on other people based on those specific values. Sometimes our values line up with those of other people and we feel mutually supported, loved and cared for. But sometimes they don't. And when other people "miss the mark," it can leave us feeling uncared for and unappreciated. Like Terri, we might find someone else's actions or behaviors exasperating because we unknowingly hold on to the belief that other people should know what we need, or at least attempt to find out.

What Matters To You

Recognizing what we value and expect is an essential part of maintaining any healthy relationship. It helps us understand why we are angry, disappointed, or frustrated by other people and it gives us an opportunity to consider how we want to proceed in a given relationship. We can choose to clarify or protect our values. Or we can decide to let something go and relegate that value to a lesser position. If our values do not align with those of another person , we also can choose to leave that relationship and pursue independence instead.

This work is especially relevant for those of us caught in patterns of codependency because:

- Sometimes we are so in tune with the needs of other people *that we become uncertain of what we value* or what matters to us.

- At other times, we spend an incredible amount of emotional energy *trying to get our needs* met by someone who cannot or will not.

- And finally, some of us have *simply given up* on the idea that an important need will ever be met and so we limp along through life without it. This is especially true in relationships with people struggling with addiction or addictive behaviors.

A Courtside Offense

Here is an example of how different values and expectations can come into conflict. Let's say you are an avid Pickleball player and you have accumulated a posse of like-minded teammates who meet on the weekends to take part in local pickup games. Learning proper technique and strategy from a winter's worth of clinics, you are confident in your game and you cannot wait to move your way up to compete at a higher level. One particular gentleman in your group is very aggressive and likes to win at all costs. He has no patience for proper technique or court etiquette. Instead, he hits the ball as hard as he can at his opponents and delights in every point he and his teammate gain. You find this behavior appalling, especially because you are often on the receiving end of his hits and you cannot stand to be around the jerk. When your group later goes out for a drink, you silently seethe in the corner of a booth and shoot daggers at him with your eyes. The offender takes no notice of you and proceeds to enjoy himself as he plans a road trip to an upcoming tournament, completely oblivious to you and your sour mood.

Now imagine that you hate the idea of giving this guy so much control over your day, so you order some well-deserved fries, summon your emotional intelligence, and begin exploring t rather unpleasant situation. You realize that behind your anger and frustration you are actually feeling sad that this on-court bully has changed the atmosphere of the game you once loved. His tactics made you insecure about your own game and afraid of humiliation (not to mention injury).

Upon further reflection, you conclude that in a relationship with other Pickleball mates you value cooperation and fun above everything else. So, you expect your teammates to be mindful of others and scale their game back when needed to avoid frightening or intimidating other people. And you might then conclude that said gentleman does not share these values and he will not meet your expectations. Like it or not, this badly behaved bloke is operating on his own set of values which are not aligned with yours.

This realization does not change your feelings about playing ball with this man, but it brings you to a more objective understanding of the situation. And as your super-charged emotions dissipate, you find yourself much more successful in deciding what you want to do about the situation, if anything at all.

Values, Needs and Expectations

Before we go any further, we should define **values, needs,** and **expectations** and see how they correlate.

Values

A **value** is simply **something that is super important to you**. You might define your key personal values as honesty, faith, and loving others, for example, while someone else might select success, hard work, and integrity. A **relational value** is **a value you consider important in order to live harmoniously with another human being**. For example:

- In a friendship, you might value <u>fun</u> and <u>adventure.</u>

- In a romantic relationship, you might value <u>physical attraction</u> and <u>spontaneity</u>.

- In a relationship with a parent, you might value <u>loyalty</u> and <u>respect</u>.

There are hundreds of different values and every person must determine what is important to them. Keep in mind that values are non-negotiable. I have no right to tell you that intellectual connection is more important than fun in a friendship. You would be remiss to insist that I should care about financial stability over spontaneity when it comes to my boyfriend. The questions at the end of this chapter will give you an opportunity to think about your important relationships and what you value. For now, you might like to consider the three relationships above (friend, romantic partner, parent) and identify one or two values that correlate for you. Here is a list of some common values to get you started. Keep in mind that this is not all encompassing.

Friendship	Parent to Child	Child to Parent	Spouse or Parnter	Colleague/Manager
Adventure	Cleanliness	Affection	Beauty	Accountability
Change	Cooperation	Affirmation	Communication	Collaboration
Commitment	Creativity	Approval	Compassion	Decisiveness
Diversity	Determination	Autonomy	Confidence	Efficiency
Fun	Education	Fairness	Connection	Flexibility
Genuineness	Frugality	Harmony	Equality	Initiative
Independence	Hard Work	Justice	Faith	Integrity
Intensity	Honesty	Loyalty	Fidelity	Intelligence
Optimism	Modesty	Perseverance	Intimacy	Problem Solving
Practicality	Respect	Privacy	Stability	Professionalism
Tolerance	Success	Wisdom	Unity	Punctuality

How Can You Live Like That?

My oldest child came into this world with a smile on his face, ready to woo any human who would interact with him. At two, when other kids in the neighborhood were riding tractors and skinning their knees, my son preferred to sit in the kitchen with me talking about music, animals and the weather. When friends or family came to visit, he asked inquisitive questions and shared his young thoughts freely, switching back and forth between English and German as needed. In later years, coaches would clamor to add my boy to their roster because his enthusiasm for other people was so infectious it inevitably sparked energy among the entire team.

Fast- forward a few years and my son was entering his sophomore year in college. After living in a dorm room the previous year, he decided he wanted a more adventurous living situation in the future. His priorities were simple: people and fun. Excited to be moving into a large, off-campus house with a handful of his fraternity buddies, he drove his packed car toward the north of our state. I followed closely behind him in nervous anticipation. The new abode was cute from the outside, a slightly run-down three-story Victorian that provided plenty of space for porch furniture and outdoor gatherings. (I imagined his Bible Study group meeting on the back lawn.) But as we opened the front door and investigated the interior, I could not hide my disbelief.

To say this was a dilapidated house would be an understatement. In fact, it had been "used" the previous summer as a venue for fraternity parties and the evidence of that was everywhere: bottles and cans were strewn or stacked on all counters, dirt and grime covered every square inch of the kitchen. The only bathroom on the first floor appeared to be out of commission but not out of use. We quickly reconsidered our thoughts about exploring the basement when we noticed a large paddle on the wall for killing bats.

As we ripped up the filthy carpet and scrubbed the floors in my son's room, I felt awful for him. I tried showering him with words of encouragement like "I'm sure it will feel like home soon" and "at least you don't have to share a room." I donned a pair of rubber gloves and scoured the upstairs bathroom making sure there was space for his toiletries. I made a mental note to buy him some patio furniture so that he could get out of the house more often.

But what I failed to realize was that my boy was delighted with his new digs. He was completely unconcerned about the grimy ring in the shower or where to place his deodorant. In his mind, this structurally unsound building provided him with a place to hang out (and live) with his people. The mess and chaos that I saw were insignificant to him considering the things he cared about: quality time, fun, conversation, and camaraderie. On the drive home later that night, I realized how differently we can see the world based on what is important to us and what we value.

Needs

A **need** is like a value and the terms are often used synonymously. A need can be described as **the emotional experience we feel when something we want or value is absent or not present**. When a singer croons, "I need love" or "I need you" it is usually in the context of not having love or the presence of a loved one at that moment. When a parent "needs respect" or "needs to be heard," it is often because they are feeing disrespected and ignored. Being able to acknowledge and express our needs is fundamental to our ability to thrive and grow in relationships, but it is not always easy. Some of us were not encouraged or allowed to express our needs as children making it difficult to identify our needs as adults. Others of us cringe at the idea of being labeled "needy" for fear that it makes us seem clingy and dependent.

Our Needs Matter

Many clients come to me saying it sounds so selfish to focus on their own needs and values. After all, we are often told to care about others and put their needs before our own. Fair enough. Sometimes, we will make a choice to set aside our immediate needs to attend to someone else's. We teach our kids to share their desserts and toys with their siblings. We encourage our employees to put in overtime for the good of the company. We ask our parishioners to support our outreach projects so that others can drink safe water and come to know God's love. There are seasons of life where we make bigger commitments to someone or some cause and give exceptionally of our time, resources and physical and emotional presence, allowing our own concerns to take the second rung.

But habitually ignoring our own values and subsequent needs is not really an act of love. Especially when:

- We fail to communicate what we need because <u>we are afraid</u> to say no.

When we refuse to set boundaries with a toddler for fear of a tantrum, we are being indulgent, not kind.

- We are <u>threatened, shamed, or bullied</u> into putting someone else's needs first.

If we cave to our partner's sexual demands for fear of being called a prude, we are not acting in love.

- We are physically tired or sick and we repeatedly <u>sacrifice our health</u> for someone else.

If we allow a friend who has "no one else to talk to" to constantly interrupt our sleep, it allows them to become dependent on us at the expense of our own health.

- We are emotionally or mentally overwhelmed by someone else's struggles and find ourselves <u>unable to show up for others</u> who are also important.

When we repeatedly arrive tired, distracted and agitated to social events because we insist on managing our parent's chaotic lives, we risk losing our sanity and our friendships.

- We <u>stunt someone else's growth</u> by doing for them something they can do for themselves (in fact, they might be better off doing it themselves).

If we repeatedly pick up the slack for a disorganized son, we waste our time, and he misses a growth opportunity.

Expectations

Our values and needs will inevitably inform our expectations. An **expectation** is a **one-sided statement about what we think or hope someone will do, say, or feel based on what is important to us**. Far more than a set of rules or regulations, expectations are simply the outcome we think should happen or the words we hope will be said. Putting this together with our values, it looks like this: If I value spontaneity, it would follow that I expect my friends to be excited when I show up unannounced. If I am received with grumbling, I might be hurt because my expectation has been dashed.

Try this sentence out with the three relationship/value combinations you came up on page 86 and see if you can define the expectation that arises from that information.

Because I value ____(*name of value*)____, I expect my ____(*type of relationship*)____ to ____(*expected behavior*)____.

For example:

Because I value <u>cleanliness</u>, I expect my <u>daughter</u> to <u>pick up her room without being asked.</u>

Because I value <u>harmony</u>, I expect my <u>parents </u>to <u>be congenial at family events.</u>

The Problem with Expectations

In recovery circles we often refer to the saying, "expectations are the root of all suffering," and as of today I cannot find an example where that is not true. Think about that statement in terms of any relationship fraught with disappointment, sadness or frustration, and you will probably find that someone has let you down because you expected them to act or think differently. If your adult child winds up in jail from a DWI, your anger with her might stem from the fact that you expected her to possess more common sense. Or you might be disappointed with yourself based on an expectation that a good parent would not produce a child who has run-ins with the law. If your mother consistently comments on your appearance, your irritation might come from a place of deep insecurity with your looks. Your expectation would be that she would speak words of affirmation and not critique you.

None of this exploration is to say we should abandon our values and eliminate expectations! To the contrary. It behooves us to become more and more familiar with our expectations so that we can understand our frequent (or maybe just occasional) sadness, anger and frustration with other people. We each need to decide individually which expectations stem from values that are non-negotiable and which ones we can manage or let go of altogether. If my mother-in-law will not stop criticizing my hair, I can decide to leave the relationship (non-negotiable value). I can also choose to ignore her (manage myself) or even laugh about her comments (let it go).

Incompatible Values, Unattainable Expectations

By the time alcoholism showed up in my marriage, I can say for certain that I was already very confused about my values, needs, and expectations. My husband and I both were. I did not possess the vocabulary to accurately articulate what I was experiencing. The addiction exposed a foundation that was not stable and lit a fire in an already volatile situation. Deeply unhappy and desperate to fix our marriage, I blamed my spouse for not wanting to join me in doing the hard work of figuring things out. He knew I was frustrated, but balked at the idea that I should label him the bad guy. In his eyes, he was a legitimately stressed-out, primary breadwinner who deserved a beer and a pat on the back when he came home (not a wife who nagged him about superfluous things like emotional intimacy). I was despondent and hopeless, and so very sad because things had started so well.

At twenty-three, I stood at the altar with a man I sincerely loved. We exchanged vows - all of which were completely heartfelt, but some of which we were both ill-equipped to keep. Like many others, we pledged to "have and hold and love and cherish." In our personal vows, we also professed our commitment to always act as a team, to have each other's backs and to grow old together. These are the sweet and tender things that people say during wedding ceremonies - phrases that get captured on video and bring tears to our eyes because there is something beautiful and captivating about a raw, unadulterated desire to love someone.

But if you had asked me at the time to write a more honest version of our vows based on the things I valued, my promises might have sounded more like this:

I will always

- say "I love you" and mean it.

- spend time with you talking, running, cooking, laughing, shopping, etc.

- resolve any conflict on the spot.

- make sure that we are more in love than any of our friends.

I will never

- have an affair.

- throw in the towel.

- be rude, mean or condescending.

- spend large amounts of money without asking you.

Those would make funny-sounding vows, but the ideas behind them are super informative in understanding what I valued at that age. I would summarize them today as my promise to provide emotional and physical connection, fidelity, and respect. Many of these values reflected the things I witnessed in my upbringing - some things I wanted to continue and other things I did not want to repeat. Notice that even though these promises reflected MY values, there is an implied understanding that HE would value some or all of the same things as well. In order for me to fulfill my vow to spend time with him, he would also need to value talking, running, cooking, laughing, or shopping together.

His vows to me would probably have sounded more like this:

I will always

- provide for you financially.

- value you as my equal.

- keep myself active and attractive to you.

- physically be there when you need me.

I will never

- ask for a divorce.

- yell or engage in a shouting match with you.

- reject or humiliate you.

- become an alcoholic.

From this list, you could extrapolate that he valued financial security, commitment, sobriety and peace. Once again, many of these hypothetical promises were in response to things he experienced in his own home: alcoholism, constant fighting and stress about finances. This was coupled with his belief that nuptials are forever and marital happiness is a matter of luck, not work. And for HIS promises to be possible, I would need to care about financial stability, unquestioned partnership, and physical presence in the same way he did.

At the beginning, our (often unspoken) needs were easy to meet - we were in love and willing to bend over backwards to make each other happy. We discussed an occasional disagreement and compromised shortly after. But as our marriage progressed, the stress of his career, several relocations, the demands of young children, and eventually alcohol addiction, tested our values. He could no longer fulfill my needs for emotional connection, healthy conflict resolution, and tenderness. To get what I needed, I resorted to forceful demands and desperate pleas for more time together, more conversation, and more love. And as my husband's addiction progressed, he became even less capable of making me happy. As a result of my behavior, he no longer experienced safety or stability in my presence.

Of course it is easy from an outside perspective to presume that the alcoholic is the culprit for creating a major rift in a marriage, and that separation from someone who refuses to quit drinking is understandable and perhaps even inevitable. (We will look a bit closer at addiction and codependency in the next section.) But the point of this chapter is not to make judgments about who is right or wrong; the message is simply that we all come into relationships with values and needs (some which we articulate and some we do not) that are not necessarily in line with those of the other person. When someone's behavior pushes up against our core values, the ones that we might call "deal breakers," it creates a relational situation that can be tremendously frustrating and maddening.

After years of fruitless conversations and hurtful accusations, I could finally come to a values-based conclusion for myself:

I need emotional connection and it is a non-negotiable value for me in marriage. I expect my partner to make eye-contact with me, spend time with me and be of sober mind when we communicate. Coming to bed drunk, canceling our dates at the last minute, and consistently tuning out of conversations are not acceptable to me. I will be supportive if he chooses to get help, but I will not continue in a partnership where my spouse is continually emotionally absent.

That may certainly sound righteous and cold. I mean, how can a marriage survive when people make demands of each other like that? But if you read that statement closely, you see it is actually NOT demanding. I am simply stating what is important to me and what I need and expect. And let me add that this work is something we do first for our OWN clarity. Whether we ever articulate it to someone else is entirely another question.

To be honest, it took a bit of work to get to where I could speak and think in a "demand-free" way. Early in the journey I said things more akin to, "I *need you* to stop drinking" or "I *expect you* to see how badly your drinking is hurting our family and stop." But in time, I recognized that his drinking was not the real problem. The core-value being stepped on was not his consumption of alcohol, it was *the absence of emotional intimacy* that resulted. From that point on, I was able to switch my focus away from controlling his behavior and instead, asking myself whether I wanted to live the rest of my life with a spouse who was disconnected.

A Look Ahead

It is entirely up to us to decide whether we protect our non-negotiable values (by setting boundaries) or if we adapt, lower, or change our expectations. Maybe that sounds frightening or a little daunting, but just consider how freeing that actually is! YOU get to choose a path forward from here that reflects what is important to you in your relationships and honors the person you were created to be.

In the next chapter, we will learn about a tool to help us deal with unmet expectations. I would encourage you to answer the questions at the end of this chapter before you continue so that you have some personal information to work with.

Reflection Questions:

1. List a few important relationships in your life, especially the ones that cause you discomfort.

- Write at least one thing you value in that relationship (using the values grid in this chapter or your own ideas). For example: mother = respect, encouragement.

2. Using the information in question one, complete the sentence below for each relationship:

Because I value ____(*name of value*)____, I expect my ____(*type of relationship*)____ to ____(*expected behavior*)____.

For example: "Because I value <u>encouragement,</u> I expect my <u>mother</u> to <u>say affirming and supportive things to me."</u>

3. Look over the statements and notice where your expectations are NOT being met.

- How does it make you feel when your expectations are not met?

- Can you imagine continuing to stay in a relationship with that person if nothing changes? Why or why not?

- Has any part of you "gone missing" because this expectation is not being met?

Further resources:

CHAPTER 6

Acceptance

"Nothing, absolutely nothing happens in God's world by mistake."
- Alcoholics Anonymous, Big Book

Before I had my own kids (when I did my best parenting), spotting a toddler in line at the grocery store used to give me anxiety. Don't get me wrong, I have always loved children and have nothing but respect for young parents who are juggling work, daycare, school, errands, naps and feedings. But the unpredictability of those cherub-faced sweethearts as they approached the candy section next to the checkout stand was enough to make my heart race. Within seconds that adorable three-year-old who was denied the green ring pop he wanted "soooo bad", could omit a shriek so piercing it was enough to make me consider forgoing motherhood altogether. And when the protests were accompanied by flailing arms and legs, even *I* was tempted to buy little junior his treat just to make the scene end.

Whenever I witness a young person lashing out at an

uncooperative world, I am reminded that we all have trouble with acceptance. As teenagers and adults, we may not throw ourselves on the ground of a retail establishment, but we have our own way of voicing our frustration when we don't get what we want. You have probably witnessed the behaviors I am referring to:

- A coach rants at a teenage umpire because she disagrees with a call.

- A manager is overly-critical and condescending toward a direct-report who mismanaged an important deliverable.

- A spouse belittles her partner for not having a higher paying job.

- A friend who did not get invited to a party uses social media to disparage others in her group.

Just for fun, look over these scenarios to see how good you are at acceptance. On a scale of 1-10 (1=rolls off my back like water on a duck, 10=would stew on this for days), rate your response:

- A car cuts you off in traffic.

- Your best friend tells you (in a moment of anger) that you are bossy.

- Your father-in-law suggests that he can teach you how to cook healthier.

- You get a (deserved) speeding ticket.

- You get looked over for a (promised) promotion.

- Your neighbor's dog poops in your yard (just once).

- Someone at work blames your political party for the decline of America.

When we talk through these situations in the workshop, most of the time people will respond by saying, "well, it depends"- it depends on my mood, how well I know the other people, if this is a repeated event, etc. That makes sense. A bit more context will always give us a more precise answer. But in general, these scenarios might give you a bit of insight into your general ability to accept situations and circumstances as they are rather than continually ruminate on issues you cannot control. You might already know if you are typically a "hot head" or whether you have the patience of an angel, or something in-between.

But before we talk more about acceptance, I always feel the need to say upfront that acceptance is not the same as resignation or passivity. It is a skill we develop that helps us decide how to react to the things that are in our control, and how to let go of the things that are not.

The Practice of Acceptance

I like to define **acceptance** as: **a decision to allow the truth about someone or something to exist while admitting we are powerless over it**. Let's break that down just a bit. First, it is a decision or a choice. It may not be intuitive for you and it may not feel good. But it is a mindset that will help you let go of feelings of resentment, anger, sadness and frustration over time and with practice. Second, when we practice acceptance, we make a rigorous commitment to seeing the truth exactly for what it is. This can be an extremely painful exercise for some of us who are dealing with difficult people and shattered dreams, but none-the-less, we cannot move forward in healing our broken relationships until we are willing to be honest about them. Finally, we admit we are powerless over people and certain circumstances. This is not to say that we allow ourselves to be repeatedly criticized or bullied or even nagged. It means that we accept our inability to change other people or situations that happen to us without our consent.

Those of us who struggle with codependent behaviors are sometimes fueled by an unwillingness to face the (often painful) truth about a person, a situation, or a relationship. When we become willing to acknowledge reality and accept our powerlessness over others, we can honestly assess what is ours to "do" and begin the path to health and healing.

Three Things We Learn to Accept

When we practice acceptance, we come to terms with three things:

1. Someone else's limitations, motivations or capacity to change.

Pamela came to coaching because her husband of twenty years had announced that he no longer had faith in their marriage and that he needed some time and space to "figure things out." Several weeks before he had packed his bags, moved in with his sister and told Pamela that he had felt horribly alone, uncared for and rejected throughout their marriage. He had reached a point where he no longer believed he was able to give her what she needed. Although Pamela did not deny that she had been a less-than-attentive spouse, she was devastated by his departure and dumbfounded that he would leave her alone to care for their young daughter (whom he was only willing to "watch" when his work schedule allowed for it).

At first, Pamela wanted to talk with me about her husband's behavior and how selfish he was. She declared her determination to fight for their marriage at all costs and as such, she continued to be there for him whenever he needed her. This included sharing meals together, going on vacation, phone conversations when he was lonely, and physical affection - whenever he asked for it. But after many months Pamela was growing weary and she was starting to believe he was in the process of leaving her for someone else.

She considered setting boundaries with him (more about boundaries in Chapter Eight) but could not bring herself to consider the idea that their marriage might be over. She begged him to go to counseling with her (which he rejected), told him she would not wait forever (which proved to be a nebulous amount of time), and appealed to his friends and family for help (who confirmed her suspicions that he had someone new). All the while she protected his secret from the rest of their community to avoid her own humiliation and his potential embarrassment.

What Pamela struggled with the most was acceptance of the truth. To everyone else it was obvious that her husband had moved on and had no intention of coming back. He was using her codependent, "good nature" to fill in the lonely hours from time to time, but in the end, he was not willing to do the hard work to reconcile (or so it appeared). In truth, Pamela's efforts of long-suffering patience and proclamations of "fighting for him" proved to be paths of avoidance. She looked up at me at the end of one difficult session and confessed that she felt like her "old self" had gone missing and that she did not like the person who had taken her place.

As we worked together, she bravely confronted her worst

nightmare: she might have to sell their beautiful house, work out custody of their precious daughter and let go of the man she loved. Those were difficult and painful sessions. Eventually, Pamela began to accept that although she was powerless over her estranged spouse, she was very much in control of herself. Once she shifted gears toward acceptance, she was able to turn her attention toward finding a way forward for herself and her daughter.

2. Our own limitations, motivations or capacity to change.

My youngest son was a collegiate distance runner. He ran for two prestigious D1 universities and earned himself many accolades including three time All-American, Big 10 Cross Country runner of the year, school record holder for the indoor 5,000 meters and three-year team captain. His junior year in college he crossed the Atlantic to win the Under 23 German National title for the outdoor 5,000 meters. He fell in love with distance running as a high school freshman and worked incredibly hard to become individual Cross Country state champion and member of the state-record-setting 4 x 800-meter relay team his senior year. Numerous articles have been written about his grit, determination and leadership, and his closet at home is filled with trophies, plaques and ribbons.

I tell you all of this not because I want to brag about my son. In truth, he achieved all of his success through very hard work and dedication, amazing teammates and coaches, and some solid running genes, that had nothing to do with me. (Although I do take credit for keeping him fed!) I share this with you because his athletic story did not end the way any of us had hoped. During his final seasons of collegiate eligibility, he began to struggle with back pain and as a result, he endured a heartbreaking and disappointing series of races. Otherwise exceptionally fit, my son would step onto the starting line and begin to feel intense pressure and fear that his back would seize up. Despite weekly sessions with a sports counselor and pre-meet relaxation techniques, he could not shake the mental demons that plagued him, and midway through his races, he often began to panic and tighten up, even when he was not in pain.

After one particularly gut-wrenching race, we sat on a wall outside the stadium together in the dark and talked for at least an hour. He was bitterly disappointed in himself but mostly, he was anguished about letting his teammates down and the others who supported him. The pressure was not subsiding and he was starting to fear that he might not be able to compete again. A few weeks earlier, a collegiate runner from another state had died by suicide and he was keenly aware that his own mental health could take a turn for the worse at any time. By the grace of God, he had the courage to begin to talk through the terrifying "what if" questions with me:

What if he quit running right then and there? What if he had to deal with the disappointment of letting his team down? What if he had to live the rest of his life knowing he failed to be the runner he had hoped he could be? What would his friends and family and supporters (not to mention his girlfriend) think of him?

During that very important night, through the painful, truth-seeking conversation, this courageous young man began to realize that he would be O.K. If he chose to end his career on the spot (which he did not), he would still be worthy and loved. His coach and team would be disappointed, but he would survive. He would definitely have a lot to grieve and the transition out of running would not be easy, but he would eventually move on. The color began to return to his face (at least what I could see in the dark) and he looked as if he had dropped a 500-pound boulder off of his back. He began to accept that no matter how badly he wanted to succeed, he had limitations. And even if others would go on to win races and titles, his path was going to look different.

Indeed, the rest of his season did not magically turn around but instead, he was able to focus less on his own performance and support and help his teammates in achieving their goals instead.

3. A circumstance or change we did not want or were not prepared for.

Kristin and Brian had been friends of ours for several years. Our lives intersected through kids, sporting events and church. We spent many weekend hours together carpooling, cheering our kids on from the sidelines, and hanging out in restaurants with other families whose lives paralleled ours. Their family seemed to have it all: a nice house in a swanky part of town, private school education, talented and well-adjusted kids, and a loving faith-community to support them. They pursued their careers, traveled, and worked out together in their spare time.

In 2008, when the global economy plunged, their lives took an equally dramatic turn. Brian lost his job and within a year they were forced to sell their home, move to a rental property and enroll their kids in the local public schools. He was devastated and understandably frustrated with the things that were beyond his control. A "mover and shaker" throughout his lifetime, he was used to getting what he wanted and doing things his way. Over time, as he struggled to find a new job, he became more and more bitter and resentful and he blamed anyone and everything for his loss.

Brian's inability to accept his situation caused considerable relational problems. His kids began to walk on eggshells around him and many friends and neighbors opted to steer clear fearing they might get stuck listening to a heated monologue as Brian ranted against the powers that be. But one person refused to cave in to Brian's poor behavior - Kristin.

I don't know whether she was simply fueled by a more positive disposition or if she had been doing work on setting relational boundaries, but either way, Kristin continued to live her life as if she had much to be grateful for. She thrived in her job, supported her kids in new and creative ways, embraced a more frugal lifestyle and stayed optimistic about the future. When the two of them showed up together, she was respectful and kind to her spouse but never indulged his complaining and resentment, often changing the subject or removing herself from those kinds of conversations altogether. Kristin also said "no" to being around Brian when he was drinking and instead, went out for a run or read a good book. Though her husband sometimes complained that she was unsympathetic to his struggles, Kristen refused to get lost in his negativity.

I cannot tell you about the health of their marriage today and I don't know if things turned around for Brian. The interesting thing for us to note is that when it comes to relationships, one person's inability to accept circumstances or change can affect not only themselves, but the people around them. When we choose to practice acceptance (instead of blame, bitterness and resentment), acknowledge our powerlessness (over people and situations beyond our control), and pursue a life of rigorous truth, our outlook can change dramatically and our relationships will have a much better chance at thriving.

Why We Struggle With Acceptance

Accepting the truth can be difficult. A significant health issue, loss of a job, the death of a loved one, or the end of a marriage can usher an overwhelming sense of instability and disorientation. For those of us who struggle with codependency or who are stuck in an unhealthy relationship, acknowledging the truth and allowing the "what ifs" to exist can be hard to stomach. This is especially difficult if the relationship involves addiction or mental illness. Here are a few reasons why we struggle with acceptance:

1. Unfulfilled Scripts

Many of us have a script that we have written for our lives. It might be a simple vision like, "I want to be at peace and be kind to others" or it might be a more fleshed out plan for your career, marriage, children etc. This script will likely reflect your values and expectations and give you a general sense of what you are striving for and what you believe a good life should look like. In Act One you might imagine yourself married, traveling the world or having a fulfilling career. Act Two might include a few children, a relocation abroad or a family-friendly home, and so on. Hear me: there is nothing at all wrong with having goals and ideals to work towards. In fact, having clarity and purpose about your calling (Simon Sinek would call this "Knowing Your Why") can help you weed out unnecessary distractions and make decisions that will honor who you were created to be.[24]

Our script becomes problematic, however, when it involves a cast of other characters. When our spouses, children, friends, extended family, and colleagues are expected to play a particular role, we may often find ourselves standing alone at center stage when the curtain goes up on opening night.

In keeping with the theater analogy, I will be the first to sheepishly admit that my children did not care for the costumes I designed for them, my spouse did not follow the lines I had written and my mom never showed up for a single rehearsal! Those expectations might sound a bit ridiculous to you, but a less mature "me" thought that I was responsible for and that I could influence everyone else's behavior. Many of us believe that it is our fault if our "people" do not speak, act, think or behave according to our plan. And so we "help" them along by constantly advising, pointing things out, and trying to get them to see things our way (otherwise known as nagging, critiquing and forcing).

In truth, we are powerless over other people's motivations, likes and dislikes, faith decisions, career choices, relationship needs, and so much more. Even in rare instances when our advice is sought or allowed, each individual will make their own choices according to the script they have written for their own life.

The Family Portrait

Acknowledging our powerlessness over others can be particularly tricky when it comes to raising children because in many ways, we are not completely powerless. It is our responsibility to protect and care for our offspring in very real and tangible ways. As they mature, part of our job is to set boundaries that are essential for their development and to allow them to experience consequences so that they will develop a sense of ownership, autonomy and a moral compass that we hope aligns with our own. But often times, we push too hard and force our will onto them because they are smaller, less mentally and verbally astute, and more easily intimidated by our power over them.

When the image that we need our children to uphold - one that feeds our egos or gives us an inflated sense of accomplishment - becomes more important than our concern for their personal development and growth, it should cause us to pause and reexamine our motives. Outside of a life-and-death emergency, I cannot think of a battle worth fighting if it erodes trust or destroys the relationship we have with our children.

Indeed, when it comes to crafting plans and scripts for our lives, we might be better off jotting things down in pencil or writing them on a dry erase board so we can adapt, edit and change course as we grow and mature and life takes its own course. Or, as a very smart friend once pointed out, I could consider letting go of my own script and instead, focus on the script that God is writing with me in it.

2. Faith-based Expectations

Over and over again, I meet with people who feel tremendous responsibility for upholding the image of a good "religious" parent, family member, friend or spouse. (Image-management is not exclusive to people of faith. Everyone is prone to wanting to look good to others.) When someone in their orbit does not perform according to their expectations, they sometimes become anxious and hyperfocused on controlling that person's behavior for fear that it might reflect poorly on them. I'm not talking about holding our kids to important moral and faith-based standards or conveying our beliefs and concerns to others when we have been given permission to do so. I am referring to the knee-jerk reaction we sometimes have to criticize, blame and shame people into submission based on our own need for approval.

- I have listened to fathers *publicly berate* their sons for a haircut (or lack of it), a clothing choice, or a season of life decision that they did not approve of.

- I have watched mothers *openly mock* their daughters for putting on too much weight claiming that "no man will ever want to marry you."

- I have met with wives who quietly *stay in abusive marriages* because they fear the rebuke of their church elders.

- I have sat with young women and men who *feel tremendous shame* about their sexual desires, believing they are somehow defective for not wanting to stay "pure" until marriage.

I am convinced that insulting, lying and coercing are not tools that align with God's will. In my understanding, more often than not, Jesus implores us to be loving, nurturing, compassionate and honest with ourselves and with each other. He repeatedly requests that we bring our broken, imperfect and willful selves into his light-filled presence so that we may examine our own hearts and our own motivations before we wag our finger or unleash our words at others. It is far more honest and God-honoring for us to admit that we need help and support in a relationship than it is to attempt to force others into submission for the sake of appearing to have things under control. While we might deceive others around us, we cannot fool God.

3. The Myth of Control

Sometimes we just don't want to admit that we are powerless. It grates against our soul to watch someone self-destruct or behave in ways that are unacceptable to our way of thinking. Historically, our western culture takes pride in promoting a positive, "can do" attitude toward life and we are told to never, ever give up. While it might be the right thing to do, allowing others to feel the pain of their own mistakes, withholding our sage advice when it is not asked for, saying "no" and removing ourselves from someone else's chaos are difficult decisions. Members of CODA, a support group for those struggling with codependency, begin their journey with Step One: "We admitted we were powerless over others, our lives had become unmanageable." The sooner we are able to admit our powerlessness over others, the quicker we will be able to turn our attention to the only thing we do control: ourselves. (See Resources at the end of the book for more info.)

WHAT I CAN CONTROL	WHAT I CAN'T CONTROL
MY ATTITUDE	HOW PEOPLE PERCEIVE ME
MY PRIORITIES	THEIR HAPPINESS
MY BELIEFS	THEIR WORDS
MY HAIRCUT	THEIR FASHION
ME	OTHERS
MY HOBBIES	HOW PEOPLE SPEND THEIR MONEY
MY BOUNDERIES	HOW PEOPLE SPEND THEIR TIME
MY WORK-ETHIC	THEIR POLITICAL BELIEFS

Grief and Loss: A Necessary Byproduct

Practicing acceptance in relationships can often lead us to experience grief and loss of various magnitudes. When we are let down by a friend, it can sting for a few days. When our spouse no longer cares about physical connection, it can hurt for much longer. Grief can be severe and sharp when it arrives unannounced or it can also be consistent and measured like a slow, dripping faucet. We call the latter "ambiguous grief" because it results in a daily loss, for which there are typically no condolence cards or sympathetic platitudes. My friend Angela tells the story of how her life was derailed when her fourth child was born with severe physical and cognitive disabilities. "I grieve every fall when kids go back to school because I know my boy will not be going with them. I grieve at every wedding knowing he will not be getting married. I grieve when I am with him and when I am not. I grieve in the morning, during the day and at night. Grief is a part of my journey and I must feel it and embrace it if I have a chance at moving forward."

Putting it All Together

Recently I was invited to a bonfire by a friend whose circle of people I had never met. After introductions and a bit of small talk, one gentleman opened the evening's festivities by making a politically-charged statement in opposition to something I care deeply about. I was caught off guard by his passion and the comments of others around him; clearly, I was the only person in the circle who strongly disagreed. Unable (or unwilling) to bite my tongue, I gently let the man know that I stood in a different political camp and then proceeded to make a lighthearted joke about my home state, claiming I had no choice but to lean a certain way. But he did not pick up on my attempt to smooth out the conversation and proceeded to let me know how misinformed my "team" was about a variety of things. I could feel the cortisol slowly coursing through my veins and made a (wise) decision to disengage from the rest of the conversation. But my thoughts kept coming back to the incident, which clearly put a damper on the evening - for me.

When I got home, I was still unsettled and decided to make a cup of tea and process a bit before going to bed. I looked over my own workshop notes and started from the beginning:

- I was *feeling* hurt, humiliated and disrespected.

- Because I *value* respect, I had the *expectation* that the man would promptly course correct after noting that his comments might be offensive, or at least hurtful to someone else.

- I decided I needed to *accept* that this man was not interested in my opinions or knowing anything about them. He was obviously charged about something *he* felt passionate about and took an opportunity to vent to a like-minded crowd (or so he thought). Nothing I could say or do was going to change his mind or even get him to engage in a more respectful way. It was likely that he had no idea how I was feeling or that his words had been hurtful.

- Although the *grief* I felt over the situation was fleeting, it still felt like a *loss* to realize that people may not care enough about me to want to hear me out. I am saddened that we seem to have lost the ability to talk about difficult subjects and approach each other with curiosity and respect.

- In the end, I made a decision to *detach* (then and in the future) and set a *personal boundary* to keep from being in that situation again. I practiced *self-care* by crawling into bed and watching a good 30 minutes of mindless TikTok videos that made me laugh. (The concepts of detachment, boundaries and self-care are covered in the next chapters.)

The unexpected benefit of practicing acceptance lies in the relief we feel when we let something go. It's like the sense of lightness we experience when taking off a heavy backpack or setting down an awkwardly shaped package that we have been carrying for too long. When we come to **accept** that we are powerless over people, places and things we can meet unpleasant realities with less fear. Instead of resisting, controlling or ignoring the things out of our control, we can admit and accept them, **grieve** our unmet expectations, experience the necessary pain and move forward.

In the next chapter we will learn how to practice acceptance, even when it feels impossible.

Reflection Questions:

1.   What did you notice about your ability to practice acceptance from the scenarios on page 100?

2. Consider a relationship that causes you pain or anger.

- What is difficult for you to accept about that person or their behavior?

- What do you need to grieve as you accept the truth about who they are or are not?

3. Think about the "script "you have written for your life.

- What things have gone according to plan? What things have not?

- Where are you struggling to get the "other actors" to comply?

- How can the tool of acceptance help you rewrite your script?

Further Resources:

CHaPTer 7

Detachment

"You're not a pit stop, Darling. I keep coming back to you 'cause you're home." - R. S.

On Valentine's Day of 2019, National Geographic released an article entitled "Nature's Clingiest Lovers."[25] Thoroughly intrigued by the title, I expected to read about the courtship of panda bears or the mating rituals of peacocks. Interestingly, the winning species was neither a fuzzy mammal nor a macho turquoise bird, but... -a fish! That's right, according to researchers, the spooky-looking, male anglerfish that lives in the deepest, darkest parts of the ocean, bites the equally terrifying female during mating. And it does not let go. In fact, "the bodies of the two amorous anglerfish fuse together, even joining circulatory systems... - (and) the male loses his eyes, fins, teeth, and most internal organs..." The male literally loses himself and becomes part of the female!

I cannot say that I find the image of this act romantic. I also wonder if the male has any prior knowledge (or instinctual intuition) that he is about to sacrifice his life. This article got me thinking about humans and how we sometimes attach ourselves, at least emotionally, to others. And although we don't lose our appendages or organs, we sometimes sacrifice our identities and our values when we simply cannot let go.

My Business or Your Business

In Chapter One, we talked about the importance of secure attachment in our early development. However, as we mature, we begin the slow and steady (and healthy) process of detaching from our caregivers and becoming more independent. In a physical sense, this means that we learn to crawl, walk and run. We wander away from our parents to play with other children and we go to school. We sleep away from home, move away to college and leave our primary caregivers altogether. But we also detach emotionally as we form and articulate our own opinions, own our own feelings, think our own thoughts, and pursue our own dreams and goals. Over time, we learn to balance our need for autonomy and self-actualization on one hand, with our desire for connection and support on the other. As discussed in Chapter Two, the ultimate goal is to achieve interdependence in our relationships; a space where we link arms with others to become the best version of ourselves.

In theory interdependence sounds blissful but in reality, it takes a bit of work to achieve. We will often wander into other people's "business" and carry burdens that are not meant to be ours. We worry and fret and sometimes obsess about others so much that it becomes difficult to detach our thoughts from theirs. Consider the last time you arrived somewhere in your car and were so absorbed in your thoughts about someone else that you could not even remember how you got there. Or, in thinking back to the previous chapter, try to recall a time you were so blindsided by someone's contrary thoughts or opinions that you could not focus on anything else for the next few days or even weeks. Even if we can accept our powerlessness over someone else's opinions, actions and thoughts, we still might find it impossible to keep our minds from wandering back to a person, an incident or a difficult situation.

Detachment Basics

Detachment is the mental action step that helps us to bring our focus and our attention back to our own lives and the things we CAN control. By engaging in a variety of detachment practices, we learn to say "no" to excessive worry and obsession over someone else's thoughts and behaviors. We also stop feeling chaotic, overwhelmed, exhausted, or anxious about someone else's life. To begin, it is important to understand that detachment is a conscious choice, but not always an instinctual one. It's hard to detach. And I cannot emphasize enough that the purpose of detachment is not to hurt, punish, or shame another person into submitting to our will. We do not dramatically announce our detachment. Nor do we turn our backs to someone with an icy stare, hoping they will "get the message" and do what we tell them to.

In most cases, we do not need to announce our detachment at all because it is a practice we master on our own. We do not withhold love, affection, or care from someone we are detaching from. As a wise Al-Anon participant once stated, "We do not detach ourselves from the person we care about, but rather, from the agony of involvement in their lives." Detachment is an intentional choice and a calm, loving decision, not a reactionary behavior toward someone else's thoughts or decisions.

A Decision to Let Go

My daughter was a bit of a late bloomer. The princess of our household, she grew up under the careful watch of two older brothers and she loved to be at home or around her family. Middle school hit her hard and like so many her age, she wrestled with feeling like an outsider. She was likable, smart and kind (says her biased mom) but physically she resembled her fifth-grade-self more than she did the other girls in her grade. Friends were often fickle. She did her best to hold tight to her posse, but often watched from the sidelines as they flirted with boys and jockeyed for position within their groups.

One evening during her sophomore year in high school, she came out of her room with tears in her eyes and shared with me how much she had been struggling. Not that she was being bullied or singled out, it was more that she felt like she didn't fit in and could not keep up. She felt uncomfortable at parties, was not interested in pursuing the boys in her grade, and was super sensitive to how other people felt about her. Although she knew it would cost her, that night she decided to "leave" her friend-group.

I was stunned that she would come to that conclusion on her own. But I was also heartbroken and nauseated at the same time, thinking about what she would have to go through. As I recalled my own friendship nightmares, my maternal instincts kicked into high gear. The thought of my little girl crying alone in her room, fearing she was about to be friendless, was overwhelming. It took everything in me to stay calm, reassure her, and tell her how impressed I was with her maturity.

On that night, I had to make a decision, as well. I knew I could not control her social life, and I also knew I could not take away her pain. Although I had fleeting thoughts of ordering "Homeschooling for Dummies," my daughter was going to figure this out herself. It would be best for both of us if I would accept my powerlessness and practice detachment. Clearly, neither of us would benefit if I stayed up worrying about her (or hatching up plans to move to a deserted island). It would certainly upset her more to see me crying, angry, or despondent about her problems. The best I could do was to stay close and connected, guide her when appropriate, and believe that she would thrive on the other side of adversity.

Confronting Our Fear

We take an enormous risk when we detach, because we are letting go of our attempt to control an outcome. In some ways, it takes a leap of faith to push through our fears and ask our brain to accept new thoughts and create new pathways. It's a bit like turning off your phone at a dinner party and removing yourself from the flow of digital conversation. After a few hours (or minutes), you might wonder if your social life will take a hit because you have not replied to messages or posts. As more time passes, you might worry that friends are upset with your lack of feedback or you could be nervous about missing an important piece of news or a trending video. Resisting the urge to steal a glance at your device and instead, keeping your attention on the people (and food) in front of you can be challenging.

But the latest neuroscience affirms that our brains can forge new pathways and create new habits with time and practice. For this reason, it is so important that we do the work of the earlier chapters so that we truly believe we have *permission* to let go.

It would be misleading to say that everything will be fine if we practice detachment: someone might fail, get hurt or make a mistake and we might not be there to stop it. Someone might struggle, suffer or be confused, and we might not be able to solve their problem for them. But that does not mean we cannot still love and support and care. Detachment means we do not attach ourselves to someone else's life because we think we can live it better for them. Many clients who have practiced detachment have found that even if they still feel sad and worried about people they love, it rarely causes them to lose sleep anymore.

Detachment in Action

The most common response from clients in practicing detachment is this: it's impossible! I just can't stop thinking about _____. Join the club! If you are like most people, focusing on anything other than a person or situation you are concerned about feels like a losing proposition. (It's a bit like the challenge of NOT imagining a white elephant after someone else tells you they can visualize one.) But like most new habits and skills, detachment requires dedication and practice. Here are a few practical things you can do to improve:

1. Go back to acceptance and grief.

When you are lying in bed at night and can't seem to "turn off" the thoughts, ask yourself, "Have I fully accepted my powerlessness over the situation and felt the grief of doing so?" This may sound like a strange proposition, but remember, if you haven't accepted the truth or felt the loss of an unmet expectation, it might be impossible to detach. Instead, you may find yourself tugged back into "control mode," agonizing over someone else's choices or scheming ways to force your own solutions.

His and Her Thoughts

Christy found herself irritated when her husband grumbled about his post-surgery weight gain. She tried to help him get out of his "funk" by cooking healthy meals and reminding him to take his physical therapy seriously. He seemed motivated at first, but after a few days, he would lose motivation and a fresh round of complaining would begin.

After several failed attempts at getting him to ditch the chips and get off the sofa, Christy realized she was trying to force her will on her hubby. Until that point, she believed she was in charge of his health. In this state of mind, it was very difficult to detach from her "problem-solving thoughts" and focus on her own needs (and those of the others in her life). Ultimately, she accepted her husband's choices and grieved the hopes she had for a healthy partner. Understanding her powerlessness helped her to remove *her* thoughts from *his* issues.

2. Remind yourself of the growth potential for the other person in the situation.

Like acceptance and grief, this is another "mindset" tool that you will want to revisit often in all of your relationships. So many of our codependent behaviors surface when we buy into the idea that pain is something to be avoided at all costs. We cannot stand to see our loved one struggling, and we feel compelled to rescue him or her. But pain can be the very thing that motivates someone initiate change in themselves or in a given situation. A motivational pep talk or a thoughtful book might inspire us to consider an alternative path. But more often than not, it takes true adversity and suffering to get us to change our trajectory. And this is where the miracle of growth happens.

In therapeutic circles we talk about "allowing people the dignity of their own suffering." Think about that for just a moment. First, we allow. This means we graciously step back and give someone permission to be in charge of their own feelings, choices and, ultimately, their destiny. Second, we consider it a dignified thing for all people to manage their own lives and their own problems. Constantly helping, advising, critiquing, taking charge and obsessing about someone can rob them of their self-esteem, which can cause someone to spiral even further into dismay. Going back to Chapter Two, think about how *you* feel when you are in a tough spot and someone tries to fix, change, or advise you without your consent. Most likely you would feel some level of irritation, defensiveness or even hopelessness on top of what you might already be going through. This does not help anyone!

Children and Resilience

Those of us who are parents or caregivers often struggle with this concept the most because we don't want our children to be uncomfortable. We instinctively want to protect them from harm and provide them with a happy, carefree childhood, which is a wonderful thing in general. But we also must acknowledge that kids need to develop courage and inner strength to become successful adults and survive in the (sometimes tough) world they inhabit.

Managing the tension between allowing and protecting is important in helping our children mature and thrive. Naturally, we should keep dangerous chemicals away from toddlers and insist that our teenagers buckle up and drive sober. But the way we react to mishaps, mistakes and times of unhappiness will inform the way our children come to face difficulties and struggles in their future. In fact, in their research on managing hopelessness and anxiety in children, Hutcherson and Williams (Chapter One) emphasize the importance of developing grit and resilience in our kids. We do so by allowing them the opportunity to face and embrace adversity, and we nurture them through it.

A Father's Dilemma

Consider this example:

Henry's high school daughter Sophie is failing biology. She is frustrated and unmotivated, claiming that dissecting frogs and learning about the cellular respiration of plants is irrelevant to her future as a Broadway theater director. She wants to drop the class and retake it online in the summer, which she claims is much more suitable for her learning style.

Henry tries to motivate Sophie by explaining how important a general education is for any career (as well as entrance to college) but she gets defensive and does not budge. Skeptical of her ability to complete a summer class successfully, Henry starts to feel unsettled. He reminds his daughter that she is pretty lazy in the summer and will miss out on time with her friends. Still, she is not moved and tells her father to leave her alone. He then takes matters into his own hands by grounding her for four weeks and checking her homework to be sure she brings her grade up. In his mind, a month of angry protests from Sophie is more tolerable than watching her fail.

Henry did what he thought was best to help his daughter succeed, and that is both his prerogative and his responsibility. Sophie may look back on this time some day and thank her father for pushing her to pass the class and not put it off until the summer. Yet it is also possible that in his heavy-handed approach, Henry blocked

Sophie from a growth opportunity.

Consider what might have happened if her father had allowed her to drop the class and face the consequences of having to pass it in the summer. She might have failed again, at which point her father still could have stepped up. But she might have succeeded, and learned something about managing time, problem solving and being aware of her own learning style. Imagine the confidence boost she might have felt if he had allowed her to advocate for herself and handle this situation on her own. Supporting and guiding our children through potential mistakes and defeats is not always easy, but at the same time, working through failures can be crucial for their growth and maturity.

3. Practice Mindfulness

Despite the way it sounds, mindfulness is the most practical detachment tool of all because it is less about mindset and more about action. When we are engaging in **mindfulness**, we decide to **refocus our thoughts to the present** or, as we say in Al-Anon, "we put our head where our hands are." Chances are, if you are struggling in a relationship with someone you desperately want to fix, change or help, your thoughts will be consumed with their issues. You might get a reprieve from such obsessive thoughts when you sleep, work, or watch TV. But as soon as your mind runs free, it floods with worry, anxiety and fear - especially if you are still trying to solve someone else's problems.

Do This Instead

When this happens, divert your attention (your head) to whatever you are doing in the present (your hands). For example, when you wake up and feel a flood of uncomfortable thoughts or concerns, decide to concentrate on what you need to accomplish in order to get ready for the day. Use your senses to smell the shower soap, feel the fibers of your towel, choose the color combination that fits your mood and savor the warm cup of coffee you just poured for yourself. Or, if you realize you have been driving your car on autopilot, lost in thought about someone's unjust behavior, intentionally shift your focus to feeling your hands as they grip the steering wheel. Look ahead of you at the make and models of the other cars on the road and take in the aroma of the Popeye's chicken bag your kids left on the back seat. When your family's request for dinner snaps you out of an unproductive mental spiral, pivot your attention to connecting with each person. Make eye contact, ask about their day, and solicit their help with the meal prep.

Do this anytime your mind wanders to useless, obsessive thoughts that you previously surrendered. As you do, you will teach your brain something important: there is no need for concern. You can survive without those thoughts. When you give yourself permission to focus on something other than a particular problem, you allow your brain to create new neural pathways. In time, the new and present thoughts will become as familiar as the non-productive ones.

Mindfulness, along with other meditative experiences like practicing gratitude, are excellent tools for general self-care, and we will discuss them more in the final chapter.

4. Repeat.

Like any new habit, learning to detach will take time, effort, and patience. At first, you might find yourself frustrated because you still can't "turn off the thoughts." Or, despite making strides in detachment, your difficult relationship does not seem to be getting any better. But eventually, you will find that the investment in focusing on healthier relationships and other things that matter to you will pay off. Most clients report they laugh more, connect better, and find more hope when they practice detachment. In her book (and app), *The Language of Letting Go,* Melody Beattie describes it best:

"Detachment is not something we do once. It's a daily behavior in recovery. We learn it when we're beginning our recovery from codependency and adult-children (children of alcoholics) issues. And we continue to practice it along the way as we grow and change, and as our relationships grow and change.

We learn to let go of people we love, people we like, and those we don't particularly care for. We separate ourselves, and our process, from others and their process. We relinquish our tight hold and our need to control in our relationships. We take responsibility for ourselves; we allow others to do the same."[26]

Detachment and Addiction

Back in high school, my best friend's older brother struggled with a cocaine addiction. Her family set up an intervention for him, which was quite progressive for the time, given that our understanding of addiction and treatment options have progressed since the eighties. Despite their petitions, he declined the offer to allow himself to be helped, and consequently, his parents asked him to leave the house the following day. A few weeks later, my friend reported that she and her mom drove past this brother as he was sitting on a street corner looking frail, emaciated and strung- out. I remember how she described the agony she and her mom felt as they continued on with their day and refused to cave in to their boundary. In a literal sense, they feared for his life, but as long as he refused treatment, there was no longer anything they could do to help him. I also remember thinking, "I could never do that."

Detaching our thoughts from someone who is battling an addiction is gut-wrenching. Whether you agree with the tough-love boundaries of my friend's family or prefer a more nuanced approach, watching someone you love deteriorate will test the mindfulness abilities of just about anyone. How can a wife think about career goals when she is wondering if her spouse is drinking himself into a stupor in the next room? What good does it do a person to enjoy an evening out knowing that their co-worker might be in an alley shooting up heroine? How can a teacher concentrate on grading essays knowing that her sister might die from a heart attack caused by an untreated food addiction?

There is no one-size-fits-all answer to these questions other than to continue to try to apply the principles of acceptance, grief and detachment as best as we can so that we thrive in our own lives as much as possible. Finding support in recovery groups like Al-Anon (and partner organizations for people who are struggling with someone else's addiction to drugs, food, gambling, sex/porn, shopping, etc.) can be life changing. In such recovery meetings, you will learn from those who have gone before you and consider options you did not think you had. (See Resource page at the end of this book.) You will probably be encouraged to think about your own behaviors and initiate change to protect your sanity. And yes, it will challenge you to practice detachment. Learning about addiction, with the help of a licensed therapist or recovery coach and finding other people to support you (and your family) can be helpful as well.

Sometimes practicing acceptance and detachment is enough to help us stop our obsession with controlling others. Other times, we need to take an additional step to set a relationship on a healthy path. In the next chapter, we will consider what it means to set boundaries to protect what we value.

Reflection Questions:

1. What is your general reaction to the concept of detachment? Rate yourself on a scale of 1-10 on how well you can detach from the problems of other people.

2. Consider your own reaction when you watch someone struggle or fail.

- Are you a rescuer or fixer? Or do you get impatient and want to take over?

- How could your behaviors be more harmful than helpful?

3. During the day, be aware of any repetitive thoughts you are experiencing regarding another person.

- Do your best to let go of those thoughts and bring your attention back to the present.

- Reflect on your experience and consider what was difficult or easy to detach from.

- Repeat the exercise for a few days (or weeks) and keep track of any progress.

Further Resources:

Chapter 8

Boundaries

"Well look here boy, I love you like family but I am not going down like that." - *Topher Payne*

You are probably familiar with the extraordinary sacrifices a neighborhood apple tree makes for the boy she loves in Shel Silverstein's 1960s classic, *The Giving Tree*.[27] Some see this book as a portrayal of the ultimate act of love; a friend repeatedly gives everything she has for the benefit of another. But others have been far more critical, pointing out that the tree caves to the boy's demands despite his lack of concern for her needs and wishes. In Topher Payne's (unauthorized) alternative ending to the book, the tree stands up for herself and says "no" to the boy's incessant requests. In addition, she lays out a few guidelines for their friendship and gives the boy an opportunity to amend his ways. Titled, *The Tree Who Set Healthy Boundaries*, Payne's version addresses a question many of us face in our codependent relationships "How much am I expected to give of myself for the sake of another?"

When I first read Payne's version of the story, I felt slightly vindicated. Among the many books we collected in our home library, *The Giving Tree* was one of my least favorite and now I understood why. Even before I knew about boundaries, I had an inkling that the boy was taking advantage of the tree's good nature and it felt wrong to promote that behavior within my own family. But there was a second, equally disturbing narrative being woven through the story at the same time: the tree was allowing it. Many of us who struggle in difficult relationships will be prone to wag our finger at "the boy" and point out the self-centered and hurtful behaviors we find impossible to condone, while at the same time, we offer our "leaves and our limbs" up for the taking over and over again.

If we want to change our codependent relationships and move forward in health and healing, we need to learn to set and maintain healthy boundaries to protect ourselves and our non-negotiable values. And the more we practice saying no, removing ourselves from unhealthy conversations, or refusing to engage in any destructive patterns of behavior, the more confident we become in our ability to find the peace and serenity we long for in all of our relationships.

Part 1: Boundaries Basics

What Are Boundaries?

The content of this chapter comes from personal and professional experience and the excellent work of Drs. Henry Cloud and John Townsend in their best-selling series, *Boundaries: When to Say Yes, When to Say No, to Take Control of Your Life.*[28] My goal is not to replicate their findings in this chapter, but rather to highlight some of their work as it applies to healing from codependency.

Per their definition, "**a boundary is something that indicates or fixes a limit or extent**." A *physical boundary* (like a fence or a wall or even our skin) provides clarity and recognizes ownership between two different places or objects. A *relational boundary* does much the same: it draws an invisible line between two different people and holds each person accountable for their own emotions, words, and actions. When someone encroaches on our relational boundary, we have several options. We can:

- ask (politely) for that person to step back from our boundary.

- tighten or fortify our boundary.

- move or change our boundary.

- allow the other person to step over (or break through) our boundary.

For example, if I value my sleep and a friend repeatedly calls after midnight, I can: request that she stop (ask), block her from calling if she does not stop (tighten), decide to accommodate a call only in an emergency (move), or put up with her calling (allow). Getting angry, feeling hurt, and/or being annoyed are certainly by-products of relational boundaries, but the choice is still mine to decide where my boundaries lie. This chapter will focus on "asking for" and "tightening" our boundaries as we make strides against codependent behaviors. But it is important to keep in mind that we have other options.

A *boundary statement* lets another person know our boundary and how we intend to protect it. Here's what a boundary statement sounds like:

- Sandy, I love driving to school with you in the mornings. But I also value my safety. When we are in the car together, I am asking you to keep your phone on the console or in your lap so you are not distracted. If you will not do that, I will find a ride elsewhere.

- Cory, going out for a drink with you is a blast. But I am uncomfortable with the crude remarks you made about women when we were together last, and I am asking you to not do that. If that happens again, I will leave.

- Pastor Anne, leading in kids' ministry is very meaningful to me and I want to continue serving the church in that way. But I feel disrespected when you habitually show up late, leaving me little time to prepare or set up. For this reason, I am choosing to step back from serving for now and will reconsider in the Fall.

- Sister, I love that you are invested in my children's lives, but as you know, I care about their nutrition and I am not comfortable with the amount of sweets they eat at your house. I am asking you to limit "treats" to once a day. If you will not respect my wishes, I will not allow the kids to come over unsupervised in the future.

In each of these statements notice that the person setting the boundary is protecting a value. (Re-read those four scenarios and see if you can identify at least one in each case.) Also, the boundary-setter is making a straightforward statement without ever using the word "boundary." Most importantly, the boundary statement includes information about what someone will do in order to protect the boundary.

Keep in mind that boundary statements are not intended to be a quick and dirty substitute for genuine conversation and conflict resolution. I simply wanted us to get comfortable hearing words that describe our needs, our requests, and our limits. We will talk more about setting up a boundary conversation later in the chapter.

What Boundaries are Not

In my experience, the biggest challenge with setting and maintaining healthy boundaries comes from misunderstanding what boundaries ARE and what they are NOT. Boundaries are NOT:

- *Impulsive.* In the heat of the moment, we are prone to say and do things that are a response to anger, fear, or hurt. While it might feel oddly satisfying to announce to your boss that you are setting a boundary and no longer sacrificing your life for his company, this kind of behavior would be more of a theatrical response to your own frustration and not an actual boundary. Boundaries are something we thoughtfully consider and communicate in a calm and empathetic way.

- *Manipulative.* I cannot emphasize this enough: the response of the other person to our boundary is not what makes it successful. Of course, we hope people will accept our limits and care about what we value, but there is no guarantee that will happen. We must be ready to give up any illusion that we can control, fix, or force someone to change because we are "getting tough" with them. A spouse who decides that he will no longer live in a marriage with someone who is emotionally abusive would certainly hope that legal separation would "force" the other person to reflect on the gravity of the situation and amend their ways, but there is no guarantee that this will happen. Here, a successful outcome would simply protect the boundary-setter from future abuse.

- *Selfish.* Saying "no" to someone we care about can feel rotten. No one likes to make someone else feel frustrated, angry or hurt. In a recent survey of workshop participants and clients, "the fear of being seen as uncaring or mean" was listed as the greatest struggle with setting boundaries. But as contradictory as it might seem, setting healthy boundaries, in love, is *good* for the other person because it gives them an opportunity to confront their own unhealthy behavior. They may not choose to course-correct immediately (or ever), but in time, they may reconsider. Also, keep in mind that setting and enforcing limits eliminates our need for nagging, pleading and over-reacting, which can be far more hurtful (and selfish) than saying "no" in the first place.

A Basic Assumption

Before we go any further, I want us to be reminded of the basic assumption laid out in the introductory chapter that continues to be paramount to this work:

You matter.

Let that sink in for a second. You matter *and* you are ridiculously in charge of yourself. Even those of us who submit to God are tasked with doing what is necessary to address areas of un-health in our lives that might get in the way of our connection with Him.

He will not do that for us, nor will anyone else. As you begin the work of setting boundaries, you might find yourself challenged by self-doubt from time to time, and that is normal. As you become more confident in your ability to control your serenity, you might find that your sense of self-worth also improves. You might also benefit from the wisdom or support of a competent therapist, trusted friend, or mentor as you embark on this journey.

Part 2: Boundaries in Action

Boundaries are perhaps the most important tool you will need to reclaim your life, your serenity and separate yourself from someone else's calamity. Setting healthy boundaries can literally mean the difference between a life marked by constant worry and pain or a path of curiosity, growth and self-compassion. But drawing a relational line between ourselves and other people can often be scary. Other people's unhappiness with our "no," "no more," or "that will not work for me," can easily bowl us over if we are not prepared.

That is why the work of the earlier chapters of this book is so important. We need to be clear about what we value and need. We need to decide what is worth protecting. We need to be familiar with practicing acceptance and detachment. Then we will be much more prepared to take action and much less prone to back down just because someone else doesn't like our boundary.

People often ask, "Will my boundary work?" Here is the truth: When healthy boundaries are correctly set, they will "work" one hundred percent of the time. That statement often solicits a great deal of skepticism from clients, who are confident that the troublesome people in their lives will not respond well to having limits placed upon them or being told "no." In fact, one of the most common misunderstandings about boundaries is that the other person has to accept, respect or respond positively to our limits in order for them to be successful. Not so. Other people have permission to be angry, sad, ambivalent, judgmental or even hostile toward our decision. They may accuse us, ignore us, throw guilt and manipulations our way or walk away quietly with a wounded air about them. The challenge for us is to remain steadfast, remember the goal, and find the support we need to withstand the discomfort.

A Tough Day

On May 15th, 2017, I sat in my counselor's office with my spouse and let him know I would no longer live with active addiction in my life. He would need to agree to treatment or move out of our home. I remember the date because it was two days before our daughter's 15th birthday and what should have been a joyful celebration became the first of many milestones he would choose not to share with his family. (My language is intentional; opting to deny his illness and refusing to get help were decisions he made that worked best for him. It took eight years of conversations, arguments, confrontations, broken promises and lies, before I finally understood my powerlessness considering those choices.)

My hands shook as I read my thoughts from a letter I had prepared and I felt strangely disconnected from my body. Was I really saying those things aloud? When I finished, I waited fearfully for him to respond, but by that time, I knew his reaction would not change my mind. It might hurt, but mostly it would inform how I was going to proceed in securing my home as an addiction-free zone from that day forward.

People who know my story often ask, "Did your boundary work?"

And to that I always answer, "yes." To this day, my children and I have lived in an honest, emotionally stable, addiction-free home. As long as that boundary is important to me, I will continue to hold fast to it. But I know well that this is not the answer most people are seeking. Understandably, they want to know if my husband responded to my boundary by getting help and whether our marriage (and family) were restored. I have shared that part of the story in the Epilogue of this book for an important reason: his response to my boundary was not essential in my choice to hold fast to it.

Of course, I prayed fiercely that he would get better and that we would eventually reconcile, and I continued to love him any way I could. But ultimately, it would be up to him to decide how he wanted to move forward. And after almost a decade of preparation, I accepted that I could no longer influence his decision by any words, pleas, tears, requests for counseling, manipulations or other actions. His choice to get sober was entirely his own.

Part 3: Setting Boundaries

Not every boundary or boundary conversation is that intense or has such high stakes. You might identify a boundary issue, have a gentle conversation and never think about it again. Or you could start by dropping a few hints, giving several reminders, or even using humor if that suits you better. *Remember, the goal of this work is to navigate difficult situations in relationships that have robbed you of your serenity, and there is no one-size-fits-all solution that works for everyone.* But regardless of the severity of the situation or the depth of the relationship, there are some basic steps I have found helpful in preparing for a boundary conversation, and sticking to those boundaries.

Preparing for a Boundary Conversation

- **Process** with a safe person to get clarity on the boundary you are setting, but don't gossip. There is a big difference between talking something through with a trusted person who understands what is at stake and venting to someone who will automatically take your side. Ask your "safe person" to be honest in their feedback and to hold you accountable when you are ready to move forward. Consider role-playing with this person so that you are prepared and calm when you set your boundary. When you encounter push-back from the person on the receiving end of your boundary, you will benefit from the support of another human to keep you focused and calm.

- **Prepare your heart.** Entering a tough conversation while angry, sad, or frustrated is a recipe for disaster. Remember that the person you are speaking with may genuinely see things differently and may not intend to hurt you. Pray, meditate, journal or talk things out with someone else in advance if you can.

- **Start small and be specific.** It's hard for someone to know how to respond to a generalized statement like, "you are always mean." Better to name a specific example like, "last week during the meeting you called me naïve..." or "this morning when I asked you to clean your room, you slammed the door in my face..."

- **Focus on unacceptable behavior,** not motivation. As tempting as it might be to call someone out for being disrespectful, rude or ungrateful, it is close to impossible to set boundaries around someone's attitude or disposition.

It is always better to name the action that is unacceptable: yelling, cursing, using unkind words, ignoring requests, hitting, gossiping, telling lies and so on.

- **Communicate well**, which includes:

  ○ Considering the best place and time for the specific person you are dealing with.

  ○ Refraining from using text or email unless absolutely necessary.

  ○ Making gentle eye contact without glaring.

- **Own what is yours**. If you have not been consistent with a boundary or have previously allowed a behavior, be sure to acknowledge that. Letting someone know you have been complicit in this issue can help to diffuse the situation and keep them from feeling like they are solely to blame.

- **Be fair and honest**. Even if you feel your boundaries are being crushed, it does not give you permission to be out of control. Raising your voice, exaggerating to make a point or using your argumentative skills to overpower someone will not help in the long run.

- **Actively listen**. This can be difficult because we believe our boundaries are necessary and fair. Keep in mind that it is normal for the person sitting across from you to have an emotional reaction or even to shut down. You can still allow them a chance to express themselves (in a non-threatening way) without giving in or changing your mind. See the next section for tips on how to respond to someone's dislike of your boundary.

- **Consider a consequence** that is reasonable and enforceable. As uncomfortable as you might feel adding a consequence, keep in mind that a boundary without a consequence is merely a request. That does not mean you have to be overly punitive or even mention the word "consequence." It simply means that you will take a next step to protect your boundary and you want the other person to know up front what it will be. For example, a colleague who engages in name-calling might be told that you will verbally address that behavior the next time it happens. A door-slamming child might be reminded they will lose screen time the next go-round. A friend who drives while intoxicated might be reported to the police.

- **Be patient.** It takes time for others to become familiar with our boundaries if we have not been in the habit of setting or enforcing them, and we might back down when the going gets tough. Learn from your mistakes and try again.

Sticking to your Boundaries: An Example

Marcus came to coaching because he felt his adult son Jason was taking advantage of him. Jason had graduated from college (paid for by his father) and was living rent-free in his father's basement while doing odd jobs here and there to make a little money. When Marcus suggested ways to find steady employment or tried to connect his son with people to network with, Jason seemed motivated for a short time but never followed through. In addition, Jason rarely pitched in around the house and never offered to help his dad with maintenance or upkeep. A man who once prided himself for being firm, fair and reasonable, Marcus was watching himself become an impatient, irritated and angry man. After being missing for fourteen months, he was ready to find himself again.

We began by identifying *respect* and *independence* as two values that mattered to Marcus in his relationship with his son. To his disappointment, he admitted that Jason did not appear to share these same values. Marcus also had to own the fact that he had allowed his son's behavior for a long time and that his repeated requests for change were unsuccessful. We thoughtfully prepared a boundary statement together and practiced having a conversation with Jason until Marcus felt he was ready.

He invited his son out for a casual dinner and, after a short time, addressed the issues. After sharing a bit of his heart and owning his own part, Marcus let Jason know that in the future, he was going to need to contribute $200 per month toward rent and $100 toward food if he wanted to continue to live in the house. He also let him know that in six months he wanted Jason to move out entirely. Finally, he told his adult son that he would need to contribute to household chores by filling and emptying the dishwasher daily, taking out the trash weekly and grocery shopping once a week. If Jason chose not to contribute in any of these areas, he would be given two weeks to find a new place to live.

Notice that Marcus did not tell Jason how he had to find the money or time to make these things happen. He did not berate him, make comments about his character, or criticize his past decisions. He simply stated that he was no longer willing to support his son in a way that was not congruent with his values. Jason now got to choose if he wanted to take his dad's (generous) offer or not. When the conversation came to a close, Jason thanked his dad for giving him a "kick in the rear" and being clear about the time frame for his "eviction". When they later arrived at home, he brought the trash bins to the curb and immediately got to work setting up networking conversations for the following week. Within the month, Jason had landed a job he loved, found a roommate, and moved into an apartment on his own. He wrote his dad a heartfelt note of thanks for everything he had done for him and hand-delivered it with a bottle of champagne to celebrate.

Wait, what? You are likely thinking there is no way your son (or anyone's adult son, for that matter) would have responded that way. And you are right! Here is the way things actually transpired:

Jason sat across from his dad and felt his face getting hot. What an ass! Did his dad really think he could come up with that kind of money? And who was he to make demands of him when he was retired and had plenty of time to do things himself? So much for "family comes first!" Too mad to argue, Jason defiantly got up from the table and walked out of the restaurant.

Marcus was disappointed (and embarrassed), but not daunted. He drove home by himself and got busy on a yard project and then called a friend to go for a walk. He left a written copy of the conversation points on Jason's bed so that there would be no misunderstandings. Jason refused to talk or interact with his dad, but by the end of the week, he completed his chores. Marcus took that as a good sign. However, the day before "rent" was due, Jason told his father he had to make a car repair and did not have the money. His father nodded his understanding and then let his son know he had two weeks to move out. A verbal lashing followed, but again, Marcus did not budge. Instead, he removed himself from Jason's presence, treated himself to a burger, and went to the movies.

During the next days, Jason tried repeatedly to sway his father, making excuses about circumstances and his tough predicament. He blamed, yelled, cried, and became despondent. Marcus listened to his son and validated his feelings, but he ended every conversation with an affirming statement: I know you can figure this out, son. On the eve of his two-week deadline, Jason threw his laptop, his clothes and his TV into his car and drove away without a word. His father collected his remaining belongings and stored them in the unfinished part of the basement. He got up the next day and began thinking of ways to convert "Jason's room" to a workout area. He was sad, but relieved.

Now, you may not agree with Marcus's boundary or the way he implemented it. In fact, you might find his detachment skills cold. The point is that Marcus set a firm, healthy boundary and stuck to it. Where Jason ended up and how he solved his problems was entirely up to him and Marcus came to understand that clearly. Obviously, hearing Jason's accusations did not feel good. Marcus was angry and hurt and spent a fair amount of time grieving. But in the weeks that followed, he continued to show resolve and use the techniques he had learned to protect something he was not willing to live without. He has hopes that one day he and his son can reconcile, but for now, he will allow Jason some time and space to mature.

More Helpful Tools

Here are a few things to remember to help you stick to healthy boundaries when someone does not like them:

- **Pain is not always bad.** Sometimes we allow people the consequences of their own actions because the pain will cause them to grow or make different choices.

- **People have permission to dislike our boundaries.** Not everyone will see things our way.

- **Drop the rope.** When someone tries to pull you into an argument or debates the merits of your boundary, you do not have to engage. Imagine yourself refusing to play "tug of war" by leaving the rope on the ground and not picking it up.

- **Actively listen, but don't respond with emotion.** Use words like "cool" (Your friend is letting you couch surf in his apartment for a month? Cool!), "bummer" (You got laid off for being late again? Bummer!) and "wow" (You are going off the grid and moving to Alaska? Wow!) when you feel the urge to meddle or control.

- **Be a broken record.** When someone tries to derail you from a boundary, repeat your boundary statement as many times as you need to. "I understand you feel your sister has ruined your life, but hitting her is not acceptable."

- **Be prepared for a response you may not like** and acknowledge your powerlessness over the other person. Remember, you don't have control over how they respond.

- **Get physical or emotional distance** when you are feeling overwhelmed. Let the person know you need some space and commit to taking up the conversation again at a later time.

- **Go back** and do the work of acceptance, grieving and detachment (see Chapters Six and Seven).

Moving Forward

This chapter has only touched on the basics of setting boundaries. Some of you might feel inspired to identify a boundary you would like to set in a specific relationship. Bravo! Remember to pull in a trusted person as a sounding board and be kind to yourself (and the other person) as you proceed. Be prepared to feel stretched and even uncomfortable along the way. Eventually, and with practice, you will probably also begin to feel strong, accomplished, relieved and even serene as you remove yourself from unnecessary worry, anxiety and frustration.

In the survey I mentioned earlier in this chapter, 76 percent of people who had set boundaries reported feeling emotionally healthier (less anger, fear, resentment and sadness), 46 percent said they stopped obsessing about someone else's problems, and 41 percent said they feel more serene and at peace. Remember to take time to evaluate your progress and consider the growth opportunities this work will afford you. I can almost guarantee that you will learn much about yourself in this process. And in time, you will feel yourself healing and your relationships improving as well.

But maybe the idea of standing up for yourself still sounds terrifying or even impossible. Perhaps you simply cannot shake the fear of the push back you expect from the other person, or maybe the boundary you need to set could lead to the severing of a relationship you are not yet prepared to end. These are completely valid reasons to put this kind of work on hold until you are ready. I would suggest that you consider finding a good therapist or coach to help you process your fears and perhaps practice setting smaller boundaries in other relationships until you feel more comfortable. Keep in mind that a myriad of factors can be at play in our readiness to be assertive or make bigger life changes. These include innate temperament, patterns learned in family of origin, current family dynamics, past trauma, financial and familial realities, and so on. There is no shame in going at a pace that works for you as long as you are moving forward!

In the final chapter, we will look at some important practices to keep your emotional tank full so that you show up well for yourself and others.

Reflection Questions:

1. What is your general reaction to the idea of setting boundaries in relationships?

2. How has the absence of boundaries in your life caused you to "go missing"?

3. Consider a difficult situation in a current relationship.

- What values of yours are being challenged by this relationship?

- What boundary statement would protect those values?

- What consequences would be appropriate?

4. Now consider having a boundary conversation with the person in Question Three.

- Go through the nine steps in the section "Preparing for a Boundary Conversation" with a trusted person - even if you are not yet ready to have the conversation.

- What is difficult about setting this boundary?

Further Resources:

CHAPTER 9
Self-Care

"I couldn't remember the last time I was kind to myself. Was I ever?"
- Sarah Ban Breathnach.

In late December 2021, I tore my right ACL in a skiing accident in Colorado. I would love to tell you I wiped out while navigating an Olympic-caliber slalom course or that I botched the landing of a helicopter jump but in fact, I was going too fast on a fairly easy hill, hit a patch of ice and bent my knee at a funny angle. With that minor transgression, I earned myself an emergency sled ride down the hill, an MRI (made tolerable by five milligrams of Valium) and several visits to an optimistic orthopedic surgeon. Agreeing on surgery to replace the missing ligament in my knee, the doctor recommended physical therapy in the interim to strengthen the muscles around the injury. Given that the surgery would be fairly extensive and the recovery long, he wanted my leg to be as strong as possible to withstand the procedure and the rehab that followed.

I was skeptical that this was necessary, but the good doctor was right. Within weeks, my quads were the envy of every patient in the treatment room. (In full disclosure, they were mostly hip and knee replacement recipients.) Both the surgery and recovery went extremely well. While I was stuck in bed, I thought about the importance of staying physically strong and healthy, considering the many mishaps and setbacks we will continue to have as we age. I was also reminded that this is true for our mental, emotional and spiritual health, as well. The more we understand and care for our "inner world," the better we will be at managing the difficulties and misfortunes ahead of us. And the more we invest in self-care, the more balanced, resolved, and serene we will be.

Part I: Basics of Self-Care

What it is and Why it Matters

Self-care and self-love have become quite the buzzwords these days. Images of people sitting in Zen-like poses at the foot of a waterfall or soaking in a luxurious tub have taken over the media channels. Marketers promise relaxation, rejuvenation and recalibration to those who will download their app, purchase their product, or register for their retreat. True, self-care can include any manner of tranquil experiences designed to quiet the mind and the body. But self-care is so much more than a momentary break from chaos. **It is a conscious decision to invest in ourselves to ensure that we are at our best for our own benefit, and for the people we care about.** It is neither indulgent nor selfish, but it is a necessary practice to help us prevent unnecessary physical or emotional meltdowns and breakdowns. People who take care of themselves are more prone to:

- build non-negotiable habits into their daily routine to support physical, spiritual and mental health.

- recognize when they are physically or emotionally "teetering too close to the edge" and do what is in their power to take a few steps back again.

- refuse to blame other people and circumstances for the way they behave or make excuses for their own poor behavior, no matter how justified they feel.

- be more content and feel a greater sense of control over their future.

The most important thing I have learned about self-care is that it is entirely my responsibility, and I don't need anyone's permission to pursue it. No one else is tasked with forcing me to slow down, manage my stress, deal with uncomfortable emotions, drink enough water, or take time out when I need it. And as good as I might be at pretending to have things under control, without proper self-care, I eventually "leak" and allow my emotions to cause harm to someone else (or to myself). Have you ever:

- snapped at your children after a long, draining day?

- turned to alcohol to rid yourself of emotional pain or unpleasant thoughts?

- cried in frustration or stomped around the house yelling about the lack of help you get with chores?

- gotten sick from too much stress or too little sleep caused by caring for someone else's needs?

- made a critical or cutting remark to your partner in a

moment of defensiveness?

- lent someone a significant amount of money although you did not want to?

- felt unsafe in someone's car and not spoken up?

- let a past resentment build to the point of bitterness?

I have done all of these things and more, for which I have had to apologize and repent. And it won't be the last time my emotions boil over or I come slightly unhinged. But there is no excuse for being consistently hurtful, rude, unsafe or bitter toward other people, no matter what the circumstances. It is my job to recognize my unhealthy behaviors, examine their roots, and make changes that bring peace back into my life.

Part II: Self-Care with Boundaries

Self-care *matters* for maintaining healthy relationships, and it is *essential* when we begin to set boundaries with people who do not have the disposition to embrace them. Addressing relational hurts or dysfunction and setting limits to protect our values is no simple task. It often requires a great deal of emotional energy to forge an alternative path for ourselves. And as you can probably attest, feeling overwhelmed, worried, or resentful about a person or a relationship can take a toll on our physical health.

When we get consumed or distracted with someone else's life, we may find it hard to sleep, to concentrate, or to find the energy to exercise or eat well. If we are not accustomed to recognizing when we are physically and emotionally depleted, our chance of successfully holding fast to our boundaries is diminished. And when we become isolated without a healthy support network, it can be very difficult to remain steadfast in the light of someone else's manipulations, accusations, or anger.

A Determined Spouse

Brooke came to coaching to understand how to live with her chronically depressed husband. She knew she did not want to end the marriage, but she also knew that she was exhausted, lonely, and constantly on the edge of tears. All her attempts to help him feel better and to motivate him to get support and professional help (including an intervention) had failed. He was not interested in finding a solution to a problem he thought he could manage, and the idea of taking medication for a "mental problem" was shameful to him. While he occasionally showed up at the dinner table or went for a walk with her in the evening, Brooke's spouse mostly lay in bed or watched TV from the sofa. He became gradually more unhappy with himself and she became more despondent.

As we began talking about self-care, Brooke was very hesitant to shift her focus from her husband onto herself. In some ways, she had grown accustomed to the cycle of codependency and unhappiness that had permeated her marriage. Assessing her own physical, emotional and spiritual health would require her to stop putting her energy toward fixing her spouse, and somehow that felt like resignation and even betrayal. She was willing, however, to address her exhaustion, and she confessed she had not slept well in over a year. Her husband's insomnia woke her up several times a night, and feeling bad about getting a solid night's rest, she got up with him. Although she did not like the optics of it, Brooke agreed that sleeping in the guest room would be helpful. To win back some of the weight she had lost, Brooke committed to having meals delivered several nights a week. She purchased a large bottle to monitor her water intake and started walking for at least half an hour every day while listening to her favorite podcast.

The results were astounding. Within a few weeks, Brooke had regained her physical strength and her brain felt less foggy. Because her spouse was often "out of it," and rarely interested in conversation or socializing, she met more regularly with friends, visited the local library, and attended church. She even signed up to serve once a month on an outreach team. Although it was strange to do so many things on her own, Brooke recognized she was capable of being alone, and sometimes preferred it. To be sure, she still had tearful days, and she grieved the loss of the man she had married along with the dreams she had for their future. But with the grief came new resolve to continue to embrace the life she was creating for herself and the people she loved. Her situation was not ideal, but she was determined to be content and grateful one day at a time, regardless of the choices her husband made for himself.

Was Brooke able to cure her husband's mental illness or recreate the life she once had? No. Did her newly found independence and resolve strike enough fear in his heart to motivate him to seek help? I honestly don't know. After six months, Brooke felt empowered and strong enough to push pause on coaching with the agreement that she would come back if necessary. What I can definitively tell you is that Brooke looked and felt better. She had more joy, engaged more freely with other people, and accepted her husband's limitations without blaming, accusing or trying to control him. Regardless of his choices, she was going to care for herself.

Part III: Self-Care Tools

There is no prescribed self-care regimen that will work for everyone, and we cannot touch on all the tools that exist to help us thrive in our relationships. Since a major part of the journey out of codependency includes self-discovery, I encourage you to approach this next section like a buffet: *put a few trusted things on your plate, but don't be afraid to try something new. Or try something again that you might not have cared for in the past. And check out what other people put on their plate - it might surprise you!*

Tools for Evaluating Our Health

In the same way you might do a wellness check-up with a physician, there are several ways to assess your mental health and commitment to all-around self-care.

1. Core Areas Inventory

Looking at several core areas of your life, rank yourself from one to ten in terms of how well you are thriving. Show with an arrow whether this area is improving or declining. Here are some examples, but you can edit these to include things that are important to you:

- Physical health (the ability to do the things I want to do)

- Relationships (quality, not necessarily quantity)

- Surroundings (positive environment at home, work, community)

- Career (enjoyment, aptitude, growth opportunity)

- Finances (stability, not necessarily wealth)

- Personal growth (improving your "inner-world")

- Joy (fun, happiness, laughter)

- Spiritual life (faith, prayer life, community)

Ask yourself: Where am I excelling? Where do I want to improve? What resources do I need to grow in a particular area? Keep in mind that you will not be at a nine or ten for everything, but you might notice areas that are in danger of depletion. Do this regularly and consider finding an accountability partner to keep you on track.

2. Daily Inventory

Do a check-in with yourself at the end of every day. Consider journaling or sharing with another person from time to time. Notice:

Your body. Does anything hurt or ache? Are you carrying stress or tightness anywhere? How are your breathing and heart rate? Are you bloated or do you have any swelling? How was your energy level during the day?

Your emotions. Do you have any lingering feelings that might be unresolved? Are you harboring any resentments or anger toward anyone? Are you worried, stressed, or confused about something or someone? Is there tightness in your chest or other signs of anxiety? Is there something you need to surrender control of?

3. Feedback

Regularly ask the people you trust how you are doing as a friend, a parent, a co-worker and so on. See if they notice any changes in your attitude or demeanor. Ask if they sense you care about them and if there is anything you can do to love or serve them better. This does NOT mean that you have to cater to the wishes of everyone, or that you need the approval of others to be content. It is simply a practice to give yourself feedback from safe people. Resist the urge to become defensive if you hear something less than positive. Instead, absorb the information and consider it thoughtfully and objectively.

Tools for Supporting Emotional Health

These are my top ten favorite tools for staying emotionally healthy. Some of them (like studying The Enneagram) are knowledge-based resources that help me understand myself and others better, which lowers my stress and anxiety. Others (like exercise) require little-to-no cerebral engagement and can be done at almost any time, offering short- and long-term benefits. This is not an exhaustive list and you will want to come up with your own set of tools that work best in caring for you.

1. FANOS. (feeling, affirmation, need, ownership, self-care)

Originally created by Debbie and Mark Laaser as a tool to help couples in recovery create a deeper sense of vulnerability, intimacy and connection, I love using this acronym to keep engaged with my emotions and needs. [29] The more often I do it, the more familiar I become with my inner-landscape and the easier it is to tell when something is not quite "right" in an interaction, conversation or relationship. At the end of the day (or any time you like), ask yourself:

- What is the one <u>feeling</u> I had today? Example: I felt excited about a new project I will be leading.

- What is one thing I can <u>affirm</u> about myself today? Example: I did a great job of listening to my child's needs.

- What was one thing I <u>needed</u> today? Example: I needed some time to myself today to organize my thoughts.

- What happened today that I need to <u>own</u>? Example: I gossiped about my neighbor at the bus stop.

- What did I do today for <u>self-care</u> or for my <u>sobriety</u>? Example: I completed a meditation.

Although it sometimes solicits a groan and an eye-roll, I have done FANOS with my kids and other friends at the dinner table and it always brings up interesting conversation!

2. Mindfulness

As we briefly touched on in Chapter Seven (Detachment), mindfulness is a part of the world of meditation and especially useful for bringing our wandering or obsessive thoughts into the present. We suspend the need to evaluate or judge any feeling we are presently having. It can be something we do from time to time throughout the day or something we build into our daily routine. We can practice mindfulness anywhere, including at work, at home or out in nature. The focus is on breathing and the awareness and acceptance of present feelings. *It is a tremendous resource to have when you want to detach from anxious thoughts or when your mind habitually "wanders" into someone else's business.* There are several good apps to help you get started, like Headspace and Calm (or Abide for a spiritual-based program). The Mindfulness Journal from leadskill.com is another great tool.

3. The Enneagram

If I had to pick one resource that has increased my self-awareness and improved my relationships most, it would be the Enneagram. While it typically falls into the category of personality tests, this tool is so much more than a stagnant report of our strengths and weaknesses. It considers our inherent predispositions (including genetics) as well as our many life experiences and assigns one of nine distinct personality types (not ranked in any order). All nine types have their own unique motivations, needs, responses to stress, and ways of interacting with other people. What I appreciate most about my journey with the Enneagram is that it has helped me understand, connect with and love other people better; especially the people who can push my buttons the most. While there are several online tests available to find your Enneagram type, I suggest the book and podcast *The Road Back to You* by Ian Cron and Susanne Stabile as a starting point.[30]

4. Mental Health Professionals

Having a therapist in my life that will listen and give helpful feedback is a non-negotiable for me. My current counselor has been a part of my self-care program for over a decade and there is no topic that is off-limits in our work together. In some seasons of life, I have seen him weekly (or even twice a week) and at other times we go for months without talking. In my personal and professional life, I have seen lives changed, marriages reconciled, relationships mended, anxiety and depression managed, and trauma healed with the help of a competent professional.

Should you decide to engage a psychologist, therapist or coach, keep two things in mind:

- Investing in your mental health requires a willingness to work hard and, sometimes, financial resources. Many health insurance plans will provide you with in-network or out-of-network options for a limited number of visits. If your desired therapist does not take insurance, and you cannot afford the out-of-pocket fees, you can inquire about a reduced rate or sliding scale. Another great alternative is to find a counseling center that employs graduate students or counselors working toward licensure. These types of "therapists in training" are typically less expensive and they bring the latest knowledge and strategies to your sessions. In addition they are supervised (outside of your sessions) by a licensed professional.

- As with any other professional, you might have to see a few people until you find a good fit. Ask your (safe) friends and family, clergy member or physician for a referral when in doubt. (See tips for finding a therapist on the Resource page at the end of the book.)

5. Gratitude

I came late to the gratitude game for one simple reason: it seemed like the dumbest thing I had ever heard. I mean seriously, my marriage was in shambles, finances were precariously unstable and my anxiety was through the roof. How would ignoring my problems and being thankful for the blue sky and the pretty birds be helpful? It felt like a mind-game, a way to trick my brain into thinking that things were not so bad after all, which seemed like a very unwise and risky proposition.

But my friends in recovery swore that the choice to be grateful could alter the way I look at my problems. They promised that I could learn to surrender control of the difficult things in my life by focusing on the beautiful parts of my life instead. So, I gave it a (reluctant) try, and in a short period, my outlook on life changed significantly. Instead of feeling like I was pretending, I actually recognized the things I had been taking for granted, and I began to more humbly offer my thanks to God. To this day, I begin (almost) every morning by making a list of ten things for which I am grateful. On tough days, it may only include things like the sun, a roof over my head and a dog that will not abandon me. On the good days, it is impossible to stop at ten.

6. Creativity

Tapping into another part of your brain (or body) from time to time can help increase overall happiness and improve mental health. It is well documented that taking part in creative acts has a calming effect on the brain and body, releasing dopamine, and dopamine works against depression. In addition, outlets like writing and drawing can help some people better navigate stress and trauma. I have friends and clients who are amazing at crafting, gardening, cooking and photography and others who prefer to create websites and social media content.

Engaging our creative side does not require any talent - it is only necessary that we enjoy what we are doing enough to leave our "regular life" for a short while and focus on something novel. I cannot draw to save my life, and most of the time I struggle to read my own handwriting. But I feel like a giddy preschooler when I have a sixty-four pack of crayons and a coloring book in front of me. There is something soothing about picking out a nuanced shade of green like "pickle" and filling in the leaves of a tree where there was once only an outline. My good friend has taken up the piano as an adult, and although he refuses to perform for anyone, the act of creating music is soothing to him. Another client brings me beautiful flower arrangements from her expansive garden.

For people who have been stuck in difficult or codependent relationships, it's hard to imagine thinking about or doing anything creative. I, too, have echoed the voices of some of my clients who had been "missing" so long that they could not remember who they used to be and what they used to enjoy. Our obsession with someone else's life choices can rob us of even the simplest pleasures, and often we don't feel like we have permission to think about ourselves. But when we re-open the door to creative thinking, and our attention is brought back to our own lives for at least a little while, the results can be life-changing. To jump start my creative thoughts, I still love Sarah Ban Breathnach's classic *Simple Abundance - A Daybook of Comfort and Joy*.[31] Each daily reading invites the reader to recall or experience very simple pleasures and creative pursuits.

7. Laughter

Even in the most difficult times, where fun and joy might seem almost irreverent, we can often find solace and relief in laughter. Some of the most meaningful funeral services I have attended ended with friends and family sitting around telling hilarious stories about their loved one's crazy antics or personality quirks. Although the tears still accompanied the laughter, most everyone benefited from the emotional release. Other times, it is our ability to laugh at ourselves that can turn a potentially aggravating situation into a more lighthearted, memorable one for everyone involved. When we confront our humanity and imperfections with humor, it can remove a great deal of stress and even guilt from our shoulders.

Perhaps it has been a while since you allowed yourself to laugh, feeling like you did not deserve it or that it might somehow negate your pain. In that case, maybe you can start small and find a joke book or a TV sit-com that once made you chuckle. Or you might spontaneously burst into self-deprecating laughter during an honest conversation with a friend. Hanging out with little kids can be a hoot, as can watching animals at the zoo. I will confess that I love TikTok videos of animals acting silly, people wiping out on slippery surfaces, and young children mimicking their parents. Figure out what you find funny (provided that it does not devalue someone else's life in the process) and take time to allow yourself to decompress with laughter.

8. Exercise

I come from a track and field obsessed family, so exercise was a required part of my life. It wasn't until I was forced to stop working out for a short period that I realized how much it had contributed to my physical, mental, and emotional health. While I sometimes attend an organized workout class, I still come back to running: it fits into my very busy schedule and does not require a lot of advance notice, equipment, or socializing. Needing only a pair of decent shoes and athletic attire, I run to get lost in my thoughts and exhaust both my mind and my body at the same time. This kind of exercise can be super helpful when I am stuck in an unhealthy pattern of thinking. When someone else's words or behavior have hurt, angered or saddened me, running gives me time and space to think things through. It allows me to relax into a rhythmic cadence that is akin to mindfulness. Best of all, exercise releases endorphins to help my overall mood. As long as my body complies, I hope to continue to run.

But I have friends who would consider running to be an act of self-hatred, preferring a less monotonous and more social workout. The point being: find something that works for you and do it. And drink lots of water when you do!

9. A Hot Shower

For me, there is something physically relaxing and mentally restorative about taking a hot shower in the evening. Call me a dork, but this little ritual is sometimes the thing I look forward to most when my day is not going particularly well. There is something magical about the combination of running water and heat that almost feels like a warm, motherly hug and a gentle pat on the head. Often, I imagine myself symbolically washing off the day - especially if it has been a hard one.

While I preferred the "dash in, dash out" version of this cleanliness ritual when it was imposed on me as a child, today it has become a ceremonial way to close out the night. I place a few candles on the sink, brew a cup of herbal tea and stream some soulful music before turning the faucet on. When I finally get in, I stand under the showerhead and let the water massage my neck and shoulders. I concentrate on taking deep breaths. As I reach for the soap and shampoo, I engage my senses by enjoying the texture and fragrance of each product. After I am squeaky clean (or when my skin puckers), I grab a well-worn, air-dried towel (more absorbent than the soft, tumble- dried ones), throw on clean jammies and hop into bed feeling calm and ready for sleep.

10. Faith

As I have already acknowledged, faith is a very personal journey. Whether you profess to belong to a particular religious group or find yourself in the non-spiritual camp, understanding your purpose here on earth and your relationship with a higher power can have certain mental health benefits, regardless of the details. The National Alliance on Mental Illness (NAMI) claims that spirituality can help improve our sense of self and give us a feeling of empowerment and connection. It can help a person "look within and understand themselves while also figuring out the greater answer to how they fit into the rest of the world." When we consider the importance of faith in navigating difficult relationships, healthy self-esteem and belief in a higher purpose can improve the way we approach others. As a Christian, my faith affects my relationships in a few fundamental ways. I believe:

- Every human I encounter is here on this earth for a reason, created by a God who loves them. Even when I am angry, disappointed, sad, or hurt, I do not have the right to behave poorly toward someone so important to God. If I am unloving toward someone, it is my job to find a healthier path.

- Humans are imperfect, but God is not. When I am struggling in a relationship with someone who has eroded my trust or ignored an important relational boundary, I might be hurt and surprised. But God is always faithful, forever loves me and wants the best for me one hundred percent of the time. When I cannot find my way in a relationship or when I seem to repel more people than I attract, my savior pulls me close and whispers, "I know. I've been there. We will get through this together."

- God can redeem any life and any situation. When I surrender my life and my will to the One who set the universe into motion and follow His lead, anything is possible. Even in the most dire situation, or when confronting the most painful outcome, I can have faith that there is a way forward toward healing and peace. I have witnessed it in the lives of others and in my own life. Even when the outcome or the answer differs from what I expected, God always comes through.

Reflection Questions:

1. Until now, what has been your understanding of the term "self-care"?

- Having read the chapter, has it changed? If so, how?

2. Think back to a time when your self-care was lacking.

- What were the circumstances that led you to neglect your physical or mental/emotional health?

- What did you learn from that time?

- How can self-care keep you from going "missing" in the future?

3. Looking over the list of self-care practices:

- Which of these might resonate with you?

- What will you add to your own list?

- Is there someone in your life who can help you stay accountable for your self-care?

Further Resources:

conclusion

"We gain strength, and courage, and confidence by each experience in which we really stop to look fear in the face... we must do that which we think we cannot." - *Eleanor Roosevelt*

Now that you have taken a few big strides into the arena of relational health, I wonder: What resonates with you? What is confusing? What seems impossible? From time to time, I like to ask my clients and workshop participants these questions. I would love to ask them of you should we ever have the chance to meet. Of course, their answers (and yours) will vary depending on the specific relational issues they are facing but two things seem to percolate to the top of the list:

- **Learning to examine and reflect on expectations is super helpful in almost any situation.** When people get agitated or upset with someone, their ability to pause, reflect and identify what they are feeling and what value is being "pushed on" can help to bring clarity. For one client, it was liberating to recognize that her brother's public criticism at their family reunion unleashed a wave of insecurity in her. In her words, "I <u>expected</u> him to talk with me in private about that issue because <u>I value being respected</u>."

- **Preparing for and role-playing a potential boundaries conversation is invaluable.** Believe me - there is nothing quite like hearing yourself say something aloud that you would normally be terrified to even think. In the workshop, participants get to hear each other say things aloud like, "no more!" and "that is not acceptable to me." The energy amongst the participants is amazing and they literally cheer and encourage each other to be bold, to push through discomfort, and to be clear and firm. It is emotional and exhausting work, but oh so exhilarating at the same time.

Theory versus Reality

There is one common concern that comes out of every workshop: *This all makes sense and it seems easy when we talk about it in theory, Sonja. But I can never actually do that. You don't know my* _____. I understand. I don't know your (spouse, child, parent, friend, family, colleague, etc.) and for sure, change can be super hard. In fact, in my experience, any big change involves an equally enormous risk. A relationship could fall apart and things may never be the same.

But think for a moment about your future. How much longer do you want to continue with the status quo? And although you may pay a price for standing up for yourself, what is it costing you (and maybe other people you love) to stay stuck where you are today? Imagine if you could harness just a little of the fire in your belly right now and be willing to try something new. Something empowering and life-giving. Something that will pull you out of a difficult or draining relationship and help you find yourself again. If that is you, I encourage you to get started today: take one step, grab a friend to encourage you, enlist the support of a coach or counselor, get a journal and start writing and speaking the truth.

Keep the goal in mind: Your personal serenity and authentic joy regardless of anyone else's choices, opinions or behaviors.

Still don't think you can do it? Let me offer you some additional data to encourage you a bit more. I asked several of my friends, colleagues and clients this question:

How has the work of setting boundaries in relationships changed your life?

Here are some things they said:

- I stopped blaming other people for my problems and instead took a hard look at the role I was playing in the relationship struggles that plagued me.

- I told my mother-in-law I would no longer tolerate her criticism and I removed myself from any conversation in which she encroached on that boundary. It was awkward, but she stopped, and now we have learned to enjoy each other's company.

- My husband and I have stopped fighting about how to live with our alcoholic adult son. We have set clear boundaries with him and when he encroaches on one of them, we follow through with the consequence he knew we would implement.

- I have so much more time to think about myself!

- I use my tools everywhere! When someone cuts me off on the highway I now think, "let it go–there is nothing you can do about it" and I really do!

- I don't get anxiety anymore when I go into a meeting with a certain colleague. Now, when he is unfairly critical, I hold up my hand, and he knows to stop.

- I am a better father and husband because I make sure my tank is filled. I nap when I need to, eat better than I used to, and exercise when I can. Best of all, I stopped feeling guilty about taking care of myself.

A Marathon, Not a Sprint

Finally, maintaining healthy boundaries and protecting our identity and our values is a lifelong journey. Like developing any new habit or skill, we must continue to practice. For some of us, this work will feel empowering, and often, others will notice the positive change. Some clients have reported that all of their relationships have benefited from improved communication and better conflict resolution. Often a family member or friend will notice that we have changed and want to know how to "get some" of the peace and serenity we have found. When one person in a family or friend dynamic pursues emotional health, it often has a ripple effect throughout a web of relationships.

For those of us who struggle with the disease of addiction, we embed these new relational strategies into a greater program of health and healing that could, in some ways, be lifesaving. The Twelve Steps of AA, for example, include "maintenance steps" to encourage program participants to be vigilant about the important new habits they are forming. In Steps Ten, Eleven and Twelve, we (paraphrased by me) continue to take personal inventory, pray for the knowledge of God's will for us and the power to carry it out, and we practice these principles in all our affairs. The founders of this program knew that the work of self-discovery and health would never be over.

I hope the same for you – that you might "find yourself" again if you have been lost or missing, that you would come to know and value yourself through a commitment to self-discovery. And that you might surround yourself with people who love and support you while protecting yourself from people who do not or cannot.

EPILOGUE

In Chapter Eight, I shared about the hard process of setting a final boundary with my addicted spouse. After many years of preparation and practice, I was ready to say no to an alcoholic marriage and ready to regain my sense of self. I missed the person I used to be, and I wanted my kids to get my best; not just my leftovers. I was prepared to file for divorce if it came to it, but I always clung to the hope that it would not. I loved my husband and still hoped he would get better. One thing I knew for certain: I was going to be fine no matter what he decided to do (or not do). I was stronger and more courageous than ever before, and I felt serene and calm.

After being "missing" for almost a decade, today I can tell you with confidence that I am back. Although my circumstances have changed, on most days I am filled with hope and at peace with myself and my relationships. I practice gratitude and detachment daily and maintain a rigorous commitment to self-care. My brain is re-learning how to think before reacting and how to "stay in my own lane" instead of assuming responsibility for everyone else. There are wonderful days and difficult ones and a lot of mediocre ones. I try to focus on living twenty-four hours at a time, and I thank God for the people who have stayed the course with me and are committed to a relationship based on honesty and authenticity.

But people still want to know how things ended up for me and my husband. I sometimes hesitate to share, not because I am unwilling or unable, but because *my* story does not have the same ending as *ours*. While the path that he chose profoundly altered my life (and that of our children), it did not keep me from pursuing an existence of joy, love and peace. Because I have had many people tell me they found hope, courage, and a sense of camaraderie after they heard the full story, I will wrap up this book by sharing those details here. Read on if you are curious, but take a pass if you would prefer.

The Ending

In July 2017, after a two-month period of separation, my husband finally agreed to get help. The weeks of being estranged from his family and living with friends had worn Rainer down. He understood our resolve would not be shaken and he surrendered the fight. After completing an addiction assessment, he agreed to residential treatment in California, completed three months of outpatient treatment in St. Louis, and immersed himself in the world of Alcoholics Anonymous. He moved back home in November of that year, just in time for Thanksgiving.

The holiday felt slightly awkward. One of our children, who lived out of state, had cut off communication with his father throughout the separation, and was not sure how to reengage. Another child who had been home from college for the summer, felt hurt and confused by his father's sudden absence. The third was still in high school, and although she had witnessed the entire ordeal unfold, she looked forward to being reunited with a sober dad. All of us, including Rainer, felt various degrees of hurt and confusion but we were also relieved and tried to treat each with grace and kindness.

Rainer and I spent the next month going on walks and sitting in coffee shops, trying to share openly from our hearts. We were both still in a great deal of pain, but at the same time we were committed to laying a new foundation for the future; one built on trust, honesty, and mutual respect. Our conversations were difficult and raw, but we kept at them and it seemed like a bit of hope had been restored. He was still too ashamed to make amends with his kids, but he had expressed a desire to do so over the upcoming Christmas holiday. It seemed like we might end that terrible year on a much better note than expected.

How many times did I ask God, "why couldn't the story have ended there?" Everyone who loved Rainer was so encouraging and wanted him to succeed. He could have been the poster child for the recovery community–another man who was brave enough to get help and a family who loved him through his illness. Everything seemed to show that we were closing a terrible chapter and moving on to something so much better.

But the positives were quickly overshadowed when he lost his job at the end of that year and then contended with several bouts of severe depression. The eighteen months that followed his unemployment felt like a roller-coaster ride through the pitch dark for all of us. Despite taking three different anti-depressants and finding various part-time jobs, Rainer was still nestled in a bed of overwhelming and ever-growing shame and fear. He paced the bedroom at night instead of sleeping, lost an alarming amount of weight, and agonized over the simplest decisions. His confidence plummeted, and he felt like he had failed us on every level. At the same time, he got careless about making a daily commitment to manage his alcoholism. His sponsor suspected Rainer had started drinking again.

On the evening of September 15 of 2019, the day after his 54th birthday, Rainer announced he needed to run an errand, drove away in his VW Passat and never came back. After a frantic night of searching for him and several conversations with the local police, two detectives showed up the next morning to confirm that they had found his car, and him, in a nearby state park. Between dusk and dawn, Rainer had ended his life.

There is nothing that can prepare you for that kind of jolt. My memory of the days that followed is still foggy, and I cannot recall all of the details. I remember sitting on the stairs off the back deck and pleading with God to "please take it back." I remember speaking on the phone with each one of my boys, hearing their sobs as they learned their father was dead. I remember my daughter coming home from school and slumping down on the floor next to me in a complete daze. I recall people were constantly coming and going, food showed up at the doorstep and someone kept handing me water to drink. I can still make out the shape of a police officer who stood in the hallway for hours. I most succinctly remember knowing that my life would never be the same.

The Path Forward

It would have been easy to become cynical. I could have questioned the value of the work I had done in acceptance, detachment and boundary setting, considering what seemed like such an egregious failure. I could have questioned my faith and asked what good it had done me to follow a God who would allow something so horrible to happen. And believe me, there were plenty of moments (that turned into days and months) where nothing at all made sense as grief took center stage. The future felt like a huge black hole and I feared I might fall into the abyss without knowing how to find my way back. How would I navigate all the decisions that had to be made when I could barely decide whether to sit or to stand?

But then the miracle was revealed to me: **I did know what to do**.

I had been practicing it for over a decade. The very tools that I had implemented during my husband's struggle with addiction would be the same tools to help me and my family move forward. I had learned how to face reality and knew that allowing immediate pain was better than running away or suppressing it. I had also learned to be in touch with my feelings and my needs. I began to accept the brutal reality of being a widow and the mother of three fatherless children. Detachment skills were crucial in focusing on the things I could control and bringing my attention to the matters at hand. Setting boundaries with others by saying "Yes, I would love a hand with the lawn-mowing" or "No, please do not come by the house right now" was such an important skill. And as uncomfortable as it felt to think about self-care, I committed to getting sleep, drinking water, eating well and meeting with friends and my therapist for emotional support.

I also learned something profound about my God. In my lowest moments, where nothing at all made sense, I felt Jesus sitting next to me, holding my hand and whispering, "I'm so sorry. I know. This is not the way it is supposed to be." As I wept, feeling exhausted and defeated, I was reminded that He came for the brokenhearted, the downcast and the grieving. With nothing else to hold on to, His grace and love would have to be enough. Day by day, sometimes through clenched teeth and fists, I made a choice to trust in His goodness, His provision, and His plan. I did not know how He would redeem this tragedy, but I held firm to the belief that He could. When it got dark and I felt unmoored, I reached out to the faithful saints He had sent to sustain us; friends, family, pastors, counselors, neighbors and so many others who supported our family when we needed it most.

And slowly, as the grief lessened over the years, I gained a clarity unlike any I'd ever experienced. Daily, I decide to believe that I am created for a purpose, loved by a God who knows me and that no situation is ever be beyond redemption. Hear me - I did not feel like this at first- far from it. But I made a choice to act "as if" and try it on for size. Now, I believe it.

Today, I am content and, on most days, serene. I have relational tools in my belt and beautiful people to lean on who give me life and encouragement. For today, that is enough.

Glossary of Terms

Acceptance A decision to allow the truth about someone or something to exist while admitting we are powerless over it.

Boundary An invisible line between two people that holds each person responsible for their own emotions, words and actions.

Codependency A relationship dynamic where one person has let another person's behavior affect him/her and who is obsessed with controlling that person's behavior.

Detachment A mental "action step" to help us bring our focus and attention back to our own lives and the things we can control.

Emotional Intelligence The ability to be aware of our own emotions, and those of others, and to manage our behavior and relationships appropriately.

Empathy The ability to recognize someone else's feelings and to understand their perspective.

Expectation A statement about what we think or hope someone will do, say, or feel based on what is important to us.

Independence A relationship dynamic where two people distance themselves from each other temporarily or permanently.

Interdependence A relationship dynamic where two people are confident and aware of each other's intentions and where honesty and truth go hand in hand with occasional sacrifice.

Mental Health The ability to understand and regulate our thought processes, feelings, fundamental beliefs and values.

Need The emotional experience we have when something we value or want is absent or missing.

Relational Template A set of unconscious rules or patterns that guide our beliefs about human interaction.

Self-Care A conscious decision to invest in ourselves to ensure that we are at our best for our own benefit and for the people we care about.

Shame The experience of feeling as if I am not enough, that there is something inherently wrong with me.

Trauma   Any experience, at any age, that leaves us feeling overwhelmed and helpless.

Value (Relational) Something you consider important in order to live harmoniously with another human being.

Resources

Support Groups for Codependency

Codependents Anonymous (CODA) www.coda.org

Al-Anon & Al-Ateen (fams/friends of alcoholics) www.al-anon.org

ACA (adult children of alcoholics) www.adultchildren.org

Nar-Anon (families and friends of drug addicts) www.nar-anon.org

O-Anon (families and friends of food addicts) www.oanon.org

S-Anon (families and friends of sex addicts) www.sanon.org

Codependency Resources

Beattie, Melody. *Codependent No More: How to Stop Controlling Others and Start Caring for Yourself.*

Beattie, Melody. *The Language of Letting Go.* (also an app)

Melody, Pia. *Facing Codependence: What It Is, Where It Comes From, How It Sabotages Our Lives.*

Addiction Support Groups

Alcoholics Anonymous (AA) www.aa.org

Narcotics Anonymous (NA) www.na.org

Overeaters Anonymous (OA) www.oa.org

Sexaholics Anonymous (SA) www.sa.org

Addiction Resources

Hazeldon Betty Ford Addiction and Mental Health Treatment

www.hazeldon.com

National Council on Alcoholism and Drug Dependence (NCADD)

www.ncadd.us

Other Support Groups

Grief Share www.griefshare.org

National Alliance on Mental Illness (NAMI) www.nami.org

Mental Health Professionals

American Psychological Association "Find a Psychologist Near You."

www.apa.org/topics/crisis-hotlines

Healthline "Nine Tips for Finding the Right Therapist."

www.healthline.com/health/how-to-find-a-therapist

Trauma

Healthline "Best Online PTSD Support Groups of 2022."

www.healthline.com/health/mental-health/ptsd-online-support-group

Crisis Hotlines (Confidential)

- Crisis Text Line   Text HOME to 741741

- National Domestic Violence Hotline   (800) 799-7233

- National Sexual Assault Hotline   (800) 656-4673

- National Suicide and Crisis Lifeline   988

- Substance Abuse and Mental Health Services (800) 662-4357

Boundaries

Cloud, Dr. Henry and Townsend, Dr. John. *Boundaries. When to Say Yes, How to Say No to Take Control of Your Life.* (spiritual)

Katherine, Anne. *Boundaries: Where You End and I Begin.* (non-spiritual)

Self-Care

"Guide to Wellness" from the Substance Abuse and Mental Health Services Administration (SAMSA) www.store.samhsa.gov/sites/default/files/d7/priv/sma16-4958.pdf

1. Sukel, Kate. "In Sync: How Humans are Hard-Wired for Social Relationships - Report from Neuroscience 2019." Dana.Org, November 13, 2019. https://dana.org/article/in-sync-how-humans-are-hard-wired-for-social-relationships/

2. Bowlby, John. A Secure Base. Parent-Child Attachment and Healthy Human Development. London, England, Basic Books Reprint Edition, 1988.

3. Sroufe, Alan. The Development of the Person: The Minnesota Study of Risk and Adaptation From Birth to Adulthood. New York, NY, Guilford Press, 2005.

4. "The Still Face Experiment. Dr. Edward Tronick." YouTube. Uploaded by TN Courts, November 9, 2016. https://www.youtube.com/watch?v=IeHcsFqK7So

5. Siegel, Dr. Dan. "Relationship Science and Being Human." Drdansiegel.Com, December 17, 2013. https://drdansiegel.com/relationship-science-and-being-human/

6. Lesperance, Alice. "Living Through Death With Harry Potter." Theatlantic.com, January 23, 2018. https://www.theatlantic.com/entertainment/archive/2018/01/living-through-death-with-harry-potter/550445/

7. Hutcherson, Will and Williams, Chinwe'. Seen: Despair and Anxiety in Kids and Teenagers and the Power of Connection. Cumming, GA, Parent Cue, 2021.

8. Lynch, James. A Cry Unheard: New Insights Into the Medical Consequences of Loneliness. Bancroft Press, Baltimore, MD, 2000.

9. Alcoholics Anonymous: The Story of How Many Thousands of Men and Women Have Recovered from Alcoholism. AA World Services, Inc., New York, NY, 2001 Edition.

10. Townsend, Dr. John. Loving People: How to Love and Be Loved. Thomas Nelson Publishers, Nashville, TN, 2007.

11. "Jerry Maguire Best Scenes: You Complete Me." YouTube. Uploaded by FilmScout, March 26, 2014. https://www.youtube.com/watch?v=jgC6VqsC3QY

12. Beattie, Melody. Codependent No More: How to Stop Controlling Others and Start Caring for Yourself. Hazelden Publishing, Center City, MN, 1986.

13. "What is Codependency?", The Recovery Village. https://www.therecoveryvillage.com/mental-health/codependency/

14. "10 Times Marie Had No Boundaries. Everybody Loves Raymond." YouTube. Uploaded by TV Land, Jul 19, 2019. https://www.youtube.com/watch?v=3qmSrn6-gCc

15. Cherry, Kendra. "5 Surprising Ways that Stress Affects Your Brain." Verywellmind.com, April 8, 2021. https://www.verywellmind.com/surprising-ways-that-stress-affects-your-brain-2795040

16. LeBlanc, Lise. PTSD Recovery Guide. Liseleblanc.com, 2022. https://liseleblanc.ca/collections/books/products/mental-health-recovery-ptsd-guide

17. Winfrey, Oprah and Perry, Bruce. What Happened to You? Conversations on Trauma, Resilience and Healing. Flatiron Books, New York, NY, 2021.

18. Van der Kolk, Dr. Bessel. The Body Keeps the Score. Penguin Books, New York, NY, 2015.

19. Thompson, Curt. The Soul of Shame. IVP Books, Downers Grove, IL, 2015.

20. Brown, Brene'. The Gifts of Imperfection. Random House, New York, NY, 2020.

21. "US Leads Overall Spend in $828 Billion Physical Activity Market." Globalwellnessinstitute.com, January 28, 2020. https://globalwellnessinstitute.org/press-room/press-releases/us-leads-overall-spend-in-828-billion-physical-activity-market/

22. Institute for Social and Emotional Intelligence. https://www.isei.com/

23. Channell, Matthew. "Daniel Goleman's Emotional Intelligence In Leadership: How to Improve Your Team." October 13, 2021. https://www.tsw.co.uk/blog/leadership-and-management/Daniel-goleman-emotional-intelligence/

24. "Know Your Why." YouTube, uploaded by Simon Sinek, October 6, 2021. https://www.youtube.com/watch?v=tF7YLGpOoz8

25. Deines, Tina. "These Animals are Nature's Clingiest Lovers." National Geographic, February 12, 2019. https://www.nationalgeographic.com/animals/article/nature-clingy-lovers-animals-news

26. Beattie, Melody. The Language of Letting Go. Hazelden Publishing, Center City, MN, 1990.

27. Silverstein, Shel. The Giving Tree. Harper Collins, New York, NY, 1964.

28. Cloud, Dr. Henry and Townsend, Dr. John. "Boundaries." https://www.boundariesbooks.com/

29. Laaser, Debbie. "Shattered Vows: Hope and Healing for Women Who Have Been Sexually Betrayed." Zondervan, Grand Rapids, MI, 2008.

30. Cron, Ian and Stabile, Suzanne. The Road Back to You. IVP Books, Westmont, IL, 2016.

31. Ban Breathnach, Sarah. Simple Abundance: A Daybook of Comfort and Joy. Grand Central Publishing, New York, NY 2009.

ACKNOWLEDGMENTS

A heartfelt "Danke Schön" to:

My book coach for reminding me that these stories need to be heard, even when impostor-syndrome said otherwise.

The team at Chesterfield Counseling Associates and the many other mental-health professionals I have come to know who work tirelessly to care for the sick, the weary and the brokenhearted.

My friends in the recovery community who have taught me the meaning of unconditional love and surrender.

The amazing pastors, leaders and staff at The Crossing Church who have fed our family physically, emotionally and spiritually.

The various circles, crews and tribes of friends and neighbors who have been "Jesus in skin," picking me up, piecing me back together and giving me time and space to heal and grow.

My sweet family. Our family tree has many unique and unruly branches (some original and some grafted) but they are all rooted in love.

My selfless partner.   You have been a source of constant encouragement, persevering through a year of endless conversations and musings about emotional health.

My clients for the sacred space we have created together.   Your vulnerability and courage inspire me every day to keep walking toward what is honorable and right.

The team of editors, illustrators, readers and supporters who have made this book and it's launch possible.

The God of love, grace and endless mercy.

Made in United States
North Haven, CT
19 July 2024

54995567R00111